To my family and friends, to my Celtic ancestors and to all the many beautiful people who have made my long years in Ireland quite magical.

Even the monarchists.

CONTENTS

ACKNOWLEDGEMENTS i
PREFACE 1
1. BLARNEY 3
2. THE BUSINESSMAN 10
3. THE GOOD DOCTOR 14
4. THE FAMILY WAY 19
5. A MAN OF SUBSTANCE 24
6. TIM THE FAITHFUL 33
7. NOBLESSE OBLIGE 39
8. MORE OF THE IRISH 43
9. THE POACHER 48
10. EXILES 53
11. CHANCERS 59
12. A DROP OF THE HARD STUFF 64
13. FACTS OF LIFE 69
14. MR NOONAN DISAPPOINTS 76
15. RANDOM EVENTS, MIRACLES AND THIN PLACES 84
16. FLANDERS FIELDS 92
17. PEOPLE AND CATS WITH NAMES 99
ABOUT THE AUTHOR 105

ACKNOWLEDGEMENTS

Thanks are due to many friends who have encouraged me to write and to all those who boosted my confidence by praising an earlier effort, *Pardonable Offences*. Being elderly, and therefore of a strictly binary persuasion, my friends are listed by gender. They include, in particular, Vivien, Peta, Pat, Mo, Jenny, Carol and Gary, Colin, Charles, Keith, Ewen, Klasie, Alf and others. I am also grateful for the comments and support of relatives including my children Andrew, Vanessa and Bridget, my brother Mick and my classicist nephew Tim. Yanina Goldenberg, my publisher, has been particularly helpful.

Photographs were taken in Ireland by Perry Leary with the exceptions of that on page 38 (Jim Hyde) and a photograph by Vivien Morgan of the author in Cascais, Portugal.

PREFACE

The Irish are known for all manner of characteristics. Foremost amongst them, over many years, has been a tendency not to stay in Ireland at all but seek fame and fortune almost anywhere else. As a result, whilst the population of the entire island of Ireland is less than 7 million (some of whom have no Irish DNA whatsoever), over forty percent of USA citizens claim ownership of at least a few Irish genes.

My own Kildare-born great-grandfather enlisted in a British regiment in about 1837 and was promptly sent to South Africa to assist in the subjugation of the proud but splendidly unruly Xhosa-speaking tribes of the Eastern Cape. He left the army after a few years and became a much respected figure and father to a large family. Until his death in 1896 he had almost no contact with Ireland or his family there.

Three generations and 95 years later my wife Patricia and I became tired of the political and social situation in South Africa and moved to Ireland whence her own Kelleher grandfather had once come.

These stories, published in two earlier books, record something of our experiences. We were treated in a kind and friendly manner from the start, even by the thieves to whom reference is made. "You are one of our own" was an often expressed sentiment.

Some of the tales here are second-hand and cannot be vouched for entirely. In many cases names have been changed in order to protect the innocent (or the guilty, as the case might be).

What a privilege and pleasure to have spent so many years amongst "my own".

1. BLARNEY

I moved to Ireland towards the end of the 1980s, bringing with me a letter of introduction to a man who, according to my Irish-South African informant, was well-known in political circles and would be able to help me obtain Irish residence and citizenship.

My first meeting with this multi-talented man took place over coffee one afternoon in a famous Dublin hotel. Thomas George Mary Daley arrived, dressed in an expensive, ill-fitting and well-worn tweed hacking-jacket and dark brown, corduroy trousers. Like his jacket, he seemed a bit weather-beaten and his face was decorated by many little star-shaped patches of distended veins that gave his complexion an interesting maroon hue. He was in very good humour and had evidently been preparing for our meeting through much of the morning by conscientiously disposing of glasses of whiskey at a smaller and less famous establishment nearby. Dr Daley was friendly and entertaining and invited me to stay at his home in the country for a few days, so that we could go into matters in more detail. His purpose, it subsequently emerged, was to determine my worth to him as a source of additional income.

The good man's home turned out to be one of many such large houses that can be found in Ireland to this day. An imposing building that had once been the rectory of a long-abandoned protestant church, it stood on perhaps five acres of land. With paddocks and an unkempt garden, it boasted a cellar that was flooded for much of the year, large rooms with high ceilings, wooden windows in need of painting and a roof that leaked when the rain came in from the southwest. There were open fireplaces in many of the rooms and an army of damp dogs, both large and small, occupied the best and warmest spots they could find every evening. Tom's children were at boarding school and so, in term-time, he shared the house with his vague wife Grace, who had an impressive, almost unquenchable, thirst for intoxicating drinks, traditional and otherwise. Her mother, a fearsome Anglo-Irish lady of 87 summers, with a voice that might knock chips off lead crystal, was also in residence. In spite of her age, she appeared defiantly vigorous and still rode to hounds, the bizarre pastime of those wealthy country folk who can find nothing better with which to entertain themselves than the harassment and torture of wild beasts. When the boys came home for school holidays, the old lady would retreat to some northern county of Ireland. There, apparently, she occupied herself, tormenting an impotent old gentleman she had known in his better days and contributing, as best she could, to the culling of the local fox population.

Thomas Daley, it transpired, was a medical graduate with a thriving country practice in the fairly remote area where he lived, perhaps some one hundred miles south of Dublin. He was, however, also a man of many talents with a complete disregard for the finer points of law, whether as laid down by the government or by the Roman Catholic church to whom, bizarrely, given his habits, he expressed great devotion. The church was still respected, even feared, in those days which were before the Irish media began to publicise the erotic adventures of Bishop Casey and some other equally rampant members of the clergy, a few of whom had rather perverse interests.

Dr Tom, as he was widely known, seemed a rare example of the stereotypical Irishman: a fictional being, really, created by English and Irish humourists and identified as being highly witty, generally benign, an inveterate liar, always idle, often drunk and seldom wise or even sensible. To some extent, Tom played up to that image. Whatever his personal failings, he expected there would be no difficulty in making an Irishman of me, given the family name and the fact that my paternal grandfather had been a son of the blood.

As evidence of his expertise in matters to do with citizenship rights, Dr Daley told me how he had managed to obtain Irish citizenship for a wealthy businessman who was completely unconnected with the country by using the good offices of a Carmelite nun and a corrupt police sergeant. These pillars of Irish society falsified documents, supporting the fiction that his client had been born to an unidentified woman in County Clare, and given up to adoptive parents who took him to Chile where he grew up. The Irish authorities were not in possession of the interesting facts that the applicant for citizenship was a wanted man in at least one country for alleged fraudulent dealings on the stock exchange and that his father was actually an Orthodox Jewish rabbi and his mother came from Latvia. Irish DNA was entirely absent but, on foot of the sworn statements of the nun and policeman, a passport was issued without much bother.

The costs of this triumph, paid for by the client, were to the benefit of the policeman, who suddenly found himself in funds sufficient to retire from the force and open a public house, and the nun, who was able to make a religious retreat in the Canary Islands every winter for the next ten years. Thomas gained from the transaction by becoming a director of his client's successful new Irish company manufacturing wheelchairs, corsets for flabby bodies and trusses for hernia control. The son of the Latvian and the rabbi soon displayed a fine passion for, and understanding of, his new country by providing regular donations in "political support" of slightly shady politicians, including a cabinet minister who was well-known for his taste in bespoke shirts and expensive wine.

I spent several weekends with Thomas Daley and was able to observe his domestic life and medical practice at fairly close quarters. Grace, his thirsty wife, was a blonde lady who must once have been both highly attractive and full of good intentions. One did not need to be specially gifted to gain the impression that something fairly fundamental had gone wrong with the Daley marriage and that she had become a member of the world's ever-expanding ranks of disappointed women. She would greet the sunrise with a double brandy, followed by a few more drinks at short intervals thereafter. She would be thoroughly relaxed, even contented, by about 11:30 of a morning.

From time to time, Grace would disappear in the direction of the stables, ostensibly to supervise grooming of the three flea-bitten horses that were kept there when not grazing in the field. Close by their stalls was a door leading to a small, poorly furnished room that was occupied by one Michael O'Shaughnessy Nolan.

Mickey was, nominally, a trainer of horses but in fact was probably not even qualified to rub them down after a ride in the rain. He was a short, red-faced man of about 50 with nice, if slightly bloodshot, green eyes and a few stained teeth that stood in his mouth like weathered fence-poles in a deserted field. He always seemed to be in muddy Wellington boots and had a small selection of distressed trousers and jackets, and an active account with the local welfare office. There was no evidence that he owned a comb or hairbrush, let alone a decent pair of leather shoes. When he spoke, I found his words musical but difficult to follow, his accent being thicker than the best of Irish stew. Whether he had ever really attempted to train or ride a horse is not recorded.

Whilst Mickey Nolan's less than fetching appearance gave no hint that he might be attractive to women, it appeared that Grace, at least, was drawn to him in some way. Possibly the image she held of little toothless Mick, blurred like an impressionist painting as her day and alcohol intake progressed, pleased her. He might have had unusually robust talents of one sort or another; possibly hidden amongst the folds of his tweeds. If so, I have no compelling evidence that it was so.

Whatever the explanation, Dr Tom was quite at his ease telling me that Grace and Mickey the trainer were "very close". Certainly, on more than one occasion when she returned to the kitchen from the stables, I noticed that she must have lost her balance and fallen over backwards onto some hay, considering the grassy remnants that were clinging to her pullover. Little Mickey never showed any signs of being inconvenienced by the arrangement, assuming that indeed one existed.

On dry days the horses were taken to a paddock about one hundred paces from the house. Water was led to a trough from a tap outside the kitchen by means of a rubber hose, perhaps one inch in diameter, set to dribble continuously so that there was no need to turn the tap on and off at regular intervals. It was simply left half-open all day. Feed was brought to the horses in the early afternoon by Tim Heenan, an odd-job man of mature years whom Dr Tom unkindly described as being "less than the full shilling" or "one sandwich short of a picnic". Timmy seemed to be a kind and friendly soul, if indeed somewhat bewildered at times. On one memorable afternoon, I returned with Tom from a visit to O'Malley's Bar, where we had been conducting an uncontrolled experiment, sampling various brands of porter for an hour or two. When we reached his home, we found that much of the rubber hose feeding water to the horses had been neatly cut into lengths. Each of these was about 24 inches long, starting just before the hose entered the trough and spaced evenly up towards the house. Water was dripping from a cut end halfway up the incline, perhaps forty paces from the tap.

Earlier that day, Timmy Heenan had gone to feed the animals and noticed that water was not running from the end of the hose into the trough. Once he had confirmed that the tap feeding the hose was in the usual switched-on position, he failed to check if there was actually a flow from the tap itself and instead concluded that there must be an obstruction somewhere along the length of the hose. He therefore decided to use the sharp end of his spade to cut open the rubber pipe in order to find and relieve the blockage surgically, as it were. He chose to start at the trough, working his way upwards, towards the house, hoping to find the problem area easily and preserve as much of the hose as possible. A rational enough approach one might say, assuming there really was a physical obstruction, but, if that were so, there was surely a fifty-percent chance it might be in the length that was nearest the house. In fact, there was nothing blocking the flow of water in the hose at all. Council workers in the road outside the Daley property had switched off the mains water supply to the old vicarage and another home nearby whilst they replaced a rusted pipe. Flow resumed while Tim was still busily slicing the pipe. Dr Daley was not in the least put out, laughed heartily and thanked him for his concern that the horses were adequately watered. A lesson in tolerance, the importance of horses in Ireland or perhaps an illustration of the sedative effects of imbibing large volumes of porter.

2. THE BUSINESSMAN

Not to be too harsh, Dr Tom Daley was essentially a liar and a thief but he was also, in the manner of the politicians and many fraudsters who shared these characteristics, great company and an entirely entertaining and likeable rogue who seemed blissfully unaware of the carnage he left behind him. His talent for planning imaginative "strokes" (scams, in modern parlance) was matched only by his inability to execute them. As one mutual acquaintance put it, he was overly ambitious, inclined always to venture "a bridge too far". Nevertheless, he somehow nearly always managed to avoid the unpleasant consequences that might follow if he offended people with access to either the police courts or to the vicious world of serious professional crime. He fell foul of the latter band of pilgrims on one occasion, making the basic mistake of offending and defrauding a man without checking his background. A due diligence study, unheard of in Tom's world, would have found his quarry had strong connections, through a cousin, to a paramilitary group north of Dublin. They, in turn, had a fine tradition of "punishment shootings" inflicted on those that annoyed them. My business partner and I were called upon to help extricate Tom and parted with a five-figure sum in order to preserve his kneecaps, or perhaps even more sensitive fittings, for a while longer. Of course this money was never repaid.

When Tom was engaged as one of my partners in a research clinic which specialised in projects that were of interest to the pharmaceutical industry, he went off on his own to the United Arab Emirates. His objective, he said, was to arrange the sale of generic medicines to a group of wealthy Arabs with whom he was friendly. He had earlier claimed to be close to a princeling from the United Arab Emirates who kept racehorses stabled about 20 miles from the Daley medical practice. So off he went, his expenses paid using our business credit card.

Tom Daley was clearly wonderfully successful in his Dubai dealings for he soon contacted us, faxing a copy of what he said was an order for numerous medicines that needed immediate delivery. To add to the excitement, the medicines required were listed in Arabic script.

According to our – previously unrecognised – top-rank salesman, an immediate and urgent requirement was for US $40,000 to be paid into his offshore bank account so that he could cover the costs of the transaction. These costs were, basically, the wholesale purchase price of the medicines and their immediate dispatch to Dubai from a friend's warehouse in London. Or so he claimed.

As ever, with well-managed frauds, a few aspects of the background story were at least partly true. Thus, Tom was indeed in Dubai, though possibly negotiating with no one more important than perhaps an Arab wine steward or a floozy in the public bar of his international hotel. Furthermore, he had certainly been known to visit the Galway Races frequented by Arab horse owners, he had a great friend who was chief executive of a generic pharmaceuticals manufacturer in London and there would naturally be a need for money "up front" to purchase drugs for export to the Emirates.

Fortunately, by the time this all took place, we had learnt, rather expensively, that although Tom was charming, he was also completely untrustworthy and untroubled by conscience. An early prototype of at least one British prime minister, it could be said. At the outset of our joint venture we, the incoming innocents, had invested a handy sum of money in the partnership. This disappeared in a matter of weeks whilst we were commuting between Africa and Ireland, moving our families. A hint as to the fate of this investment was given by a sudden upgrade in the standard of motor vehicles possessed by the Daley household. Tom also saw fit to replace his slightly threadbare hacking jacket with a bespoke coat from an upmarket Dublin tailor. Reason enough, therefore, to treat the information from Dubai with a degree of care if not outright cynicism.

The Arabic script was remarkably untidy looking. One could not help believing that, particularly in a country that banned the recreational use of alcohol, an order involving an alleged expenditure by the buyers of well over US $100,000 would be set out in a neat and professional manner by a sober and capable individual. So the suspect "order" from the Emirates was taken to our local hospital and handed for translation to an Iraqi doctor that we knew. He was told no more than that this was an urgent message from someone in Dubai whom we wished to help. When he read it, the expression on his face was wonderful to behold. The poor man thought he was being made a fool of. "Why did you ask me to read this?" he said. "It is just a shopping list for groceries." No orders for aspirin, penicillin or digitalis, then.

Of course, nothing further developed and Dr Tom returned from the Middle-East tanned, bearing several bottles of duty-free alcohol, as jovial as ever and quite unembarrassed by the failure of his attempt to pull a stroke on his partners. Had the money been transferred, he would have claimed that the drugs had been delivered and subsequent failure to receive payment and profits would have been blamed upon the Arabs. The US $40,000 would have remained in his account, naturally.

A warm and amusing man of unusual and much wasted talents was Tom Daley. As most people know, the dominant Christian sect in Ireland offers consolation and conditional absolution to its large flock of imperfect men and women and these services are provided with added enthusiasm when handsome fees are involved. If the Roman dogmas are justified and absolution can indeed be purchased, Tom Daley could, in time, find himself, to his wide-eyed wonder, joy and astonishment, in a perfect paradise, presumably equipped with a new liver and a clean conscience. If not, he will surely be much in demand as a spinner of fireside tales by others who share one of Dante's circles with him in the other place. Meanwhile, his body lies as quietly as those beside him in a churchyard beyond the hills to the north of the Deise.

3. THE GOOD DOCTOR

Tom Daley operated his moderately busy medical practices from surgeries in two villages near his home. His standard practice was to send anyone who consulted him and seemed even slightly ill to the local hospital. He confided in me, after doing justice to a full bottle of Burgundy, that he had never considered himself a gifted diagnostician and, rather like the matron at my old school, felt that anyone who looked sick and did not respond to reassurance or an aspirin should be seen by a competent hospital doctor or nurse as soon as possible. Sometimes he treated a few of his older patients in person, but only if he considered them to be basically well and in no immediate danger.

On one occasion, I accompanied Dr Tom on a home visit to such a patient. He was an old fellow who lived with his wife in a decaying thatched cottage some five miles down the road. Pat O'Keeffe, as he was named, suffered from the respiratory consequences of smoking 40 cigarettes daily for 60 years. Before we left the Daley house, Tom loaded some bulky equipment into the back of his vehicle. One item was an easily identifiable large, metal cylinder that, according to the label on its side, contained 100% oxygen. Attached to it was a peculiar-looking device that I did not recognise. This, Tom kindly explained, was a veterinary hood, normally used to resuscitate distressed, newly born horses or cows and that it would be a perfect channel for delivering oxygen to his patient. A novel approach perhaps but, purely by chance, just what the patient needed. Dr Tom was unaware that individuals with what is now called chronic obstructive pulmonary disease do badly if given pure oxygen and must be treated with an admixture of oxygen and air. However, the size of the veterinary hood, far greater than that of a man's head, was such that a near perfect mixture of room air and oxygen was likely to be delivered to the patient. Thus treated, Pat O'Keeffe survived the crisis and lived to fight another day. Ignorance can indeed be bliss.

On another occasion I witnessed an attempt by him to draw blood for laboratory analysis from a patient's large forearm vein. My impression was that, even after more than 25 years in practice, he remained totally unable to master the simple technique involved. A few years later, I was told by a respected surgeon of his vintage that, *inter alia,* Tom had distinguished himself at medical school by competently relieving the students' union of its funds and gathering together a group of morally relaxed women of a certain age to attend to the baser needs of his classmates on the occasion of their graduation party. Versatile in at least some respects he most certainly was.

Thomas, a most hospitable man, would take me to various village pubs in the vicinity of his home, there to regale me with stories of what he regarded as his past triumphs which generally provided insights into his slightly warped world view. Subsequent events should perhaps have been foreseen, had I taken his tales of larceny more seriously, but until then I had no personal experience of either sociopaths or pathological liars. Tom was fond of planning various subterfuges with the objective of separating others from their assets as painlessly (to himself) as possible. When justifying his petty crimes, he would either say, "We were both over twenty-one," or point out that the Hippocratic Oath he had taken on graduating from medical school proscribed neither chicanery nor indeed fraud. Like an inveterate gambler at the races, he was happy in his work and admired those who were his peers or betters at the game. He evidently slept well, whether thanks to the good offices of a fine Irish whiskey, absolution by his priest or perhaps a complete absence of any conscience. He seemed to me invariably contented and, at times, even slightly euphoric.

Thomas Daley paid few, if any, taxes for decades. In time, he was collared and had to sell his practice and home to settle unpaid tax bills and penalties, as well as pay the fees of the barristers who helped him secure a fine rather than a custodial sentence.

It was not long before he distinguished himself in dubious circumstances once more. He moved away from his home in the south of Ireland to live in the relatively empty rural area to the west, where he became "medical adviser" to a foreign charlatan named Professor Milo Zumpt. This was a man who, in earlier times, would have been described as a salesman for "snake oil" and a total fraud.

Zumpt, whose background was difficult to pin down, possibly because Bulgarian criminal records are not that easy to access, offered miraculous cures to men, women and children suffering from terminal cancer.

Desperate people would somehow find large sums of money, usually amounting to thousands of pounds, only to be prescribed enemas containing coffee or herbs and to be given, for an extra financial consideration, "light therapy". The latter involved confining the unfortunate patient for two hours in a rough wooden box which had been fitted inside with a string of Christmas-tree lights bought at some flea-market. Of course, the "light therapy" had no effect. On the other hand, the coffee enemas caused anxiety symptoms and cardiac irregularities due to the absorption of dangerous amounts of caffeine from the bowel mucosa. Dehydration and salt imbalances resulted from the frequent bowel actions associated with the enemas and helped to hasten the demise of Zumpt's, by now penniless, patients.

Epidemiologists would have found no need to resort to mathematical modelling in order to describe the likely outcomes at this *faux* cancer clinic. There was a steady, 100% mortality rate. In fairness, Dr Daley was himself almost entirely without medical knowledge or expertise and it is just possible that he actually believed in Professor Zumpt's claims himself.

After a year, numerous complaints and revelations in the newspapers brought investigators to the "treatment centre" and criminal charges were laid against the principals. Dr Tom brought all his skills to bear once more and avoided becoming a guest of the state, this time by giving evidence against Milo Zumpt. The self-styled professor was deported after a short stay as a guest of the Irish government in a suitable institution. The patients were buried or cremated.

Thomas Daley disappeared from the scene whilst Zumpt was in custody and died in obscurity not long thereafter from an unfortunate, chronic liver complaint. As was customary in Ireland, his funeral mass was well-supported by family, drinking companions, debtors, creditors and an impressive selection of priests. Dr Tom would have approved of the many falsehoods that were stitched together in the eulogy spoken from the pulpit on this occasion. In his defence, one might quote the line from an old Jewish joke: "His brother was worse".

He was a man who, in spite of (or partly because of) his almost complete lack of conscience, added more than his fair share to the general gaiety of life in and about his stamping grounds: the ultimate lovable rogue.

4. THE FAMILY WAY

There were reasons to believe that Dr Tom Daley's unusual and arresting character, or perhaps *nature* would be a better word, was at least partly due to an unfortunate and unasked for variable in the arrangement of his genes. He suffered from an inheritedly disability that was not immediately obvious to the untrained eye and which science has linked to certain behavioural aberrations.

Certainly a number of his siblings had their own peculiarities, none more so than the youngest of his three brothers, Eamon.

Some years before my arrival in Ireland, Eamon Daley became a medical student at one of the better Irish universities, even though his record in high school had been rather patchy. His father's connection to several influential local politicians and businessmen probably did him no harm and he was admitted to college without any difficulty. A common enough occurrence during times when, if rumour is to be believed, school-leaving certificates and driving licences could easily be bought on the black market.

Eamon enjoyed his social life at medical school to such good effect that, instead of completing the course in six years, he was still a very undistinguished clinical student there after nine years had passed. He devoted his time – happily, it should be said – to carousing and hell-raising; a veritable legend amongst the younger students and, naturally enough, the nurses. During his tenth year, shortly after making an unfortunate mistake in one of the teaching hospital's operating theatres, Eamon's consistently idle behaviour came to the notice of the medical school management and it was decided that direct action was called for.

During their clinical training, students were expected to attend a certain number of surgical procedures as observers and, suitably prepared and scrubbed, to watch proceedings from the outer fringes of the small group of doctors and nurses gathered around the patient in the operating theatre. They would, occasionally, be asked to assist the nurses in one way or another. During one such operation, conducted by an eminent gynaecologist as it happened, Eamon was asked to take a dish containing a surgically removed sample of human tissue to the sluice room. There it was to await sectioning and microscopic examination by a pathologist who would determine precisely what abnormality was involved and whether disease might spread to other organs.

He took the specimen into the sluice room where he was almost immediately distracted by the pleasing sight of a pretty junior nurse who was busy cleaning the stainless-steel surfaces there. Understandably preoccupied by lust, he placed the dish on the sill below an open window, dislodging its cover as he did so. Wasting no time, he approached the nurse and whilst he was occupied trying to negotiate an entertaining evening, his back to the window, a large seagull swooped in from a neighbouring rooftop and flew off with the tissue, leaving behind an empty, bloodstained dish. The young nurse, facing the window at the time, witnessed the bird's theft and became hysterical. Astonished by what he took to be her response to his attempt at beguiling her, Eamon feared for a moment that he had finally lost his touch. Whatever her response might ultimately have been, the subsequent reactions of the theatre sister and, most notably, the gynaecologist and pathologist, proved to be his undoing.

Shortly after this incident, his father and eldest brother were summoned by the university authorities and invited to accept a generous offer that had been prepared for Eamon. If he would undertake to leave the country and promise never to return to practise as a doctor in Ireland, he would be allowed to graduate. He would be expected to keep his end of the bargain by moving to somewhere far afield such as Tasmania, Botswana or Afghanistan – or indeed, anywhere else that was more than a day's march from Ireland.

At the start, it is probable that the newly graduated Dr E Daley had every intention of keeping his word, or that of his father and brother, to be exact. He left Ireland for Australia where he registered at a doctors' locum agency. This office specialised in finding temporary employment for acceptably qualified foreign doctors who were in demand in both the private and public sectors of medicine. A popular posting was as *locum tenens* in a practice where one of the partners was away for postgraduate training, or on leave for some other reason. The agency doctor would usually be paid a handsome salary and could often stay free of charge in the home of the man he was replacing.

Eamon proved to be an effective *locum tenens*, partly because of the happy coincidence that it was summer in Australia and most potential patients, at least in rural communities, were in rude good health and had no need of medical attention. This state of affairs continued for about a year and no complaints were made against him with regard to his professional services. Then, alas, a Dr Bruce Jones returned home from Singapore where he had attended an eight-month postgraduate course in tropical diseases.

Dr Jones found that, medically speaking, his practice was in very good order but, to his considerable dissatisfaction, that both his wife Joan and daughter Maureen were several months pregnant. There was, needless to say, only one clear suspect in the case, namely the rampant Dr Eamon Daley, the locum, who had been living in Dr Jones' home during his absence. Wisely but ungallantly, the bold Irish rover vanished overnight, taking the first available flight to Europe.

An altogether interesting scenario resulted after the usual incubation period had passed. Dr Jones' wife, Joan's, new daughter Sylvia and her older daughter Maureen were clearly half-sisters. Maureen's baby son Fred was, of course, Joan's grandson but this made Joan's new daughter, Sylvia, and her grandson, Fred, not only half-brother and sister (through Eamon) but also aunt and nephew. At far more than a single stroke, the bold Dr Daley became both the biological father of Fred and Sylvia but also, in one sense, Fred's step-grandfather. All achieved before reaching the age of thirty.

One can only hope that no unfortunate congenital infirmity was transmitted down the generations in the process but my confidence is not at all great and it is impossible to be certain that this tale is true since it was told to me by Tom Daley himself.

5. A MAN OF SUBSTANCE

Birds of a feather flock together, or so the saying goes. Otherwise expressed, this adage translates directly as "like attracts like". A kind of reverse of the way magnets act. So, when looking back today with clearer vision it should have been obvious to me that other disturbed, dishonest or unconventional individuals might well enter the picture during my brief collaboration with Dr Thomas Daley.

Dr Tom was certainly a charming, unreliable, erratic, not to say shambolic, and amusing rogue. He was forever attempting to achieve a financial "stroke" somewhere on the outer fringes of what was legal but was doomed nearly always to fall prey to far more accomplished villains who had greater measures of talent and ruthlessness than he did. He was rather like a jackal that survives on whatever scraps can be found once the larger and fiercer predators have had their fill. Tom kept to the shadows, always ready to make good his retreat in an instant if necessary.

One day, a few years before the advent of the Celtic Tiger, Tom telephoned me with the exciting news that he had met a wealthy South African professional man in Guernsey who might be willing to invest much needed funds in our research laboratory, at that time a struggling joint venture. Dr Daley, unfortunately, was so excited by the potential for easy money that this new "best friend" seemed to offer that he failed to remember the old advice – that the Channel Islands should best be seen as sunny places filled with shady people. An invitation was issued to Tom's well-heeled new friend to visit us at the clinic and, in due course, Gerry Steyn came to lunch.

Gerry, who claimed to be the English-speaking and liberal-minded relative of a former Governor General of South Africa, made an excellent first impression. He was well-spoken, perfectly groomed, clean-shaven with a conservative haircut, wore polished shoes and was dressed in an immaculately pressed, double-breasted suit that appeared to be the product of expert tailoring in London or Paris. Much later we were to learn that he was inspected and then sent forth each day by his gifted, Svengali-like, wife and co-conspirator, Anna. She would cut his hair and eyebrows, brush his coat and buff his shoes regularly, to make quite sure that he always looked perfectly groomed. She was something of a seamstress too and took great care to stitch around the edges of his suit lapels to give them, at least at first glance, a bespoke appearance, disguising the fact that they had actually been bought off the peg in a bazaar. A range of ties and cufflinks, chosen for their superficial resemblance to those of famous clubs, regiments or universities, completed the convincing picture of an elegant man of substance.

A preliminary business agreement was reached during that first luncheon together and, making full use of contacts and friends of the Daleys, Gerry Steyn was soon installed *en famille* in an empty section of a large country house in Kilpatrick, the country seat of a respected and unsuspecting Anglo-Irish baronet. Gerry's young son attended the nearby junior school and Anna assisted now and then at a feeding scheme for the indigent of the county. The Steyns also made sure they were seen regularly in devout mode at the local parish church.

Looked at in retrospect, it might be said that Gerry followed a fairly simple protocol, building a house of illusions brick by brick, day by day. He would attend public gatherings briefly to determine whether any well-known people were present and try to overhear their conversations or exchange a word or two whilst passing by with a drink. Even if he had not spoken to any prominent people, he would mention the names of such individuals strategically during later conversations with those he planned to impress and eventually to rob. Phrases such as, "When I was at the Galway Races with Bishop Casey," or, "The Papal Nuncio is a great lover of Mozart, you know," uttered by a confident, well-dressed man worked wonders in Catholic Ireland. Of course this technique was just a minor variation of that used by salespersons of one kind or another almost any day in Britain or further afield. Lies such as, "You will really enjoy wearing it; my sister has three of them," or, "We can resurface your driveway with a load of tar we have left from Sir George Smedley's place over in Potters Bar," come to mind. Gerry would also be sure to mention his current, albeit temporary, address which he had carefully and deliberately chosen to add to his carefully manicured aura of wealth and respectability. Such simple techniques, designed to put the intended victims of any scam at their ease, work well for much of the time. Furthermore, very few busy people would be bothered to check any of the references that he chose to use, something he relied upon.

Where Gerry differed from scoundrels with more modest ambitions, such as Thomas Daley, was that he always made detailed plans and followed them carefully and to the letter; he prepared at length. During the previous months he had considered the options open to him in Europe and, learning that very few fraudsters were ever imprisoned in Ireland (there being few, if any, police investigating such crimes at the time), decided that the country of saints and scholars would provide an ideal setting for what he had in mind.

It was always his preference to defraud large companies and particularly banks rather than just the average man-in-the-street. This was not for reasons of compassion or morality but simply because he was not interested in stealing small sums except on those rare occasions when he needed a few hundred pounds to finance his next great move. It was to that end that he first built up the image of total respectability from which he could operate. A dapper appearance, an impeccable address, *faux* business cards and frequent superficial references in the right company to his eminent "friends" and to his love of operatic or symphonic music, wine and literature all helped the cause. It was only some months after he suddenly and quietly disappeared from Ireland that the full extent of his infamy came to light. Whilst he was in residence in a wing of the Kilpatrick manor, nobody suspected that this well-mannered and generous host was an utter scoundrel.

When all of this took place, South Africa was in turmoil and a significant number of businesses shifted investments, or their offices, abroad. Within the country it was relatively easy to obtain loans on limited security if the bank manager could be persuaded that the money was to be invested in local projects. To finance his plans, Gerry borrowed money from three quite separate Johannesburg banks. He did this for the obvious reason that drawing down a single large amount from one source could possibly arouse the suspicions of financial controllers in the country who might then interfere with his plans. His persona and his patter were so convincing that none of the managers performed due diligence tests; after all, he was an educated white man who made a good impression and the individual loans were not that large.

Once the money had been deposited and he had secured three different credit cards, one from each bank, Gerry began preparing for his next move which was to be the translation of his family to Ireland with certain of their movable assets. Whilst still in South Africa, using local credit cards, he leased three new cars from different motor companies. He chose two luxury saloons of German make and a top-of-the range Japanese estate vehicle. In each case, to impress the salesmen with his affluence, he paid three months rental in advance, financed with money loaned by his banks. Using the same tactics, Gerry collected solid oak office furniture "for my new export offices" from a gullible supplier. He also spent a modest sum on a large crate of choice South African wines that would come in useful if and when he entertained his chosen "victims" in Ireland.

Quite whom he bribed within South Africa is unknown, but somehow Gerry obtained permission to move his cars, furniture and wine to Ireland, "temporarily". Two cars were placed in storage some miles from his accommodation in Kilpatrick. He drove one of the expensive saloons, a BMW 5-series, as he went about his daily business in and around the area, making the right impression just as the economy began to expand. All three vehicles were heavily insured but, for reasons that became apparent much later, only against fire and theft.

Whilst Gerry was working quietly on his master-plan, he was also establishing himself in the local community. His young son made his mark at the local school and his wife cultivated her neighbours. He let it be known that he was a keen chorister and joined a group of largely devout but innocent and unsuspecting local individuals who were preparing to perform Handel's Messiah later in the year. Whether Gerry had much in common with the choirmaster is not recorded. Lady choristers of a certain age were said to be impressed by how freely he wielded his baton. A reference, one should assume, to the wand with which he conducted the ensemble. Even so, he did resign as "court musician" rather suddenly and without explanation.

Gerry's parents came to visit on one occasion and his father, claiming to be the pastor of a non-conformist church somewhere in the Transvaal, was invited to preach, in the interests of ecumenism, at the ancient Anglican cathedral nearby. Perhaps it is unfair to speak of this as an instance of "like father, like son" but at least one cynic noticed remarkable similarities between "Pastor" Steyn's homily and a sermon delivered by Martin Luther King some 25 years earlier. Nevertheless, the Steyns were soon accepted in polite society, just as Gerry had intended.

Once he had been introduced by Dr Tom Daley to a number of shady individuals in Dublin and Cork who would cooperate with his plans, Gerry went seriously to work. Firstly, he engineered a minor collision with a van on a busy road near Kilpatrick, making sure it was witnessed by several people whom he impressed by graciously refusing to make an issue of the incident. He did, however, arrange to have the small dent in his rear fender repaired in Dublin rather than at the perfectly adequate garage near his new home. At the time this seemed like an inconvenient way in which to deal with a minor problem but, of course, an agenda had already been agreed by Gerry and his co-

conspirators, of whom Tom Daley was the chief.

The almost brand new BMW had been heavily insured against fire and theft. It disappeared mysteriously from the Dublin garage without trace and was duly reported stolen. The insurance company paid out a large sum of money to Gerry which he accepted with good grace. He also collected seventy-five percent of a smaller fee paid by the Dublin-based Albanian thief who had acquired the car, driven it away from the garage and spirited it by ferry to Eastern Europe for resale at a large premium. The remaining funds went to the cooperative garage owner who had left his premises unlocked for an hour or two to facilitate the robbery.

The next steps included opening bank accounts in Ireland and the Isle of Man, as well as the sale of a second leased luxury car to another well-dressed, slightly shifty-looking Balkan gentleman. The latter met Gerry in a Waterford hotel, carrying a valise stuffed with British currency. Naturally, no registration papers changed hands on that occasion.

Once his personal bank accounts were well in the black, Gerry was able to acquire gold credit cards, each with generous credit limits. He continued to follow his plans and, preparing to move on from Ireland, consolidated his financial position at the expense of all and sundry. He sold his oak office furniture to a neighbour for a few hundred pounds together with the last bottles of wine that remained in his cellar. In addition, he took care to remain at least two months in arrears in all his accounts, including rental. His landlord was naturally perturbed by this sudden change in behaviour but far too genteel and polite to press him.

Meanwhile, Thomas Daley had not been rewarded for a peripheral part he had played in arranging the disappearance of the BMW and became impatient. He explained to Gerry that he might soon be making the acquaintance of a rather unpleasant and unsympathetic enforcer if he did not hand over the agreed share of the takings.

Time for the immaculate man of substance to preserve his knee-caps and move on.

Soon afterwards, Gerry and the entire Steyn family disappeared without trace. Well after the banks had closed, the day before they left Ireland, Gerry drew funds from a series of automated teller machines within a 30 mile radius of Kilpatrick. He went to the limits of his credit cards, thereby leaving all his current accounts well in debit. The computer programmes used in banking were by no means as sophisticated then as now and his action in withdrawing funds rang no immediate alarm bells. He was therefore able to leave the country with negotiable bank notes worth a great deal, none of which had actually been honestly earned.

Late in the evening, the day before they left Kilpatrick, the estate car was packed with the Steyns' clothes and other essentials. The latter included selected stolen items that would be useful negotiable assets: a painting, some silver, an antique mirror and two oriental rugs, all liberated from the landlord's rented property. They drove away before first light, heading for the ferry at Rosslare. From there they travelled to Wales and after further rapid, pre-arranged transactions such as the sale of the estate car, the rugs, items of silver and the painting, boarded a flight for South Africa where they would remain for some years, out of reach.

When an Irish police sergeant searched the vacated premises at the back of the old Kilpatrick manor, he discovered no less than three lapsed identity documents stuffed in a black rubbish bag together with other papers, including demands for immediate payments from various lenders and businesses in four different countries. Whether the official documents were very high quality forgeries or genuine passports obtained by some clever subterfuge was never established. Gerry was variously identified in the three passports as Gerhardus Johannes Steyn, Gregor Johan Stein or George Isaac Stone. Dates of birth and residential details were not consistent, either. Presumably he left Ireland and returned to South Africa on foot of yet another document.

A scoundrel of some ability and not without personal charm, Gerry's final stroke was played perhaps eight years after the events described here. He sent his son back to Kilpatrick to tell anyone there who was still interested in pursuing him that his father had died suddenly and unexpectedly in South Africa.

An unlikely story perhaps and no doubt a prelude to his next adventure in some other country.

6. TIM THE FAITHFUL

Whatever might have been written, Dr Thomas Daley did not limit himself entirely to exciting activities such as fraud, drinking Jamieson's best whiskey or pimping for his friends. He could be quite helpful in some ways, especially when the effort involved fitted in with his hidden agenda, one which usually involved the separation of a fool from his money. He advised me that the quickest way in which to become integrated into Irish society was to buy a house in the country, spend time there and make friends amongst the local population. Not nuclear science, perhaps, but sound advice even so. He asked what type of environment I favoured and when hills, woodland and perhaps a river were mentioned, he became quite animated. "I think I know the place," he said.

Next day, we headed across a ridge of high hills to the south of Tipperary, the Knockmealdowns, and travelled to that part of Waterford County known as the Deise. We entered a small town in the Blackwater Valley and set about finding an estate agent. The main street was no more than 300 paces in length so that proved easy enough.

The premises occupied by the man we needed to consult consisted of two inter-leading rooms in a building that had probably seen its best days in about 1802. The entrance area and front office were poorly furnished, high-ceilinged and could be accurately described as offering more character than comfort. The bare floor appeared well-scrubbed and a few of the oak boards were stained and slightly warped, presumably as a result of leaks and spillages of some kind. At least two finely constructed spider-webs occupied corners of the high ceiling which, though dusty, was almost white. There was a waist-high, battered old wooden counter along one side of the room. It had been painted a few decades earlier in less than harmonious shades of cream and green and was covered with buckets of water containing cut flowers of different kinds. The surface acted, as it turned out, as a work bench for the estate agent's wife, a florist. A cloud of smoke originated from the general area of the counter, obscuring the wall behind it on which a large framed print hung; when the fog cleared a bit, we could identify it as being of a thoroughbred horse and a small colourful fellow, presumably a jockey.

Seated behind the foliage, cigarette in hand, was a comfortably upholstered, jovial-looking man of perhaps 58 summers. He introduced himself to us as Timothy J. Hegarty. Later, on enquiring about his reliability, people invariably spoke of him as "a great man", a favourite phrase in Ireland. There was plenty of evidence that Tim was undoubtedly a force for much good in the local community and beyond.

Within days of our first meeting, Tim helped me to find and purchase my Irish home, an old Georgian pile where I live to this day. Later, he was to prove a charitable, honest and very good friend. A devout Christian, he might best be remembered as Tim the Faithful.

Some months later, during the week after Christmas, my wife and I came to live in the old house near Lismore for the first time. Tim took us around town to meet the main characters, especially those from whom we might buy essential provisions. Most memorable of the first introductions was to one of Tim's contemporaries and oldest friends, the delightful Michael Madden, who ran a small grocery shop on the high street. It was possible to pass through the front of the shop and enter seamlessly into a public house behind it but still be under the same roof. Madden's Bar was one of about a dozen on a street of no more than 30 doorways. The proprietor was quite extraordinarily kind to us, not only supplying what we needed by way of groceries but also, to our astonishment, asking if we could use an advance of fifty pounds, the banks being closed for the holidays at the time. He also warned us gravely that we should avoid the local market town, Dungarvan, as it was "littered with chancers and gobshites".

Some weeks later, we learned from the same dear man, Michael the Generous as he became known to us, that he could recall when almost every shop in town had a pub attached to it like that behind his grocery store, and that one such hybrid had been owned by the local tailor. If a young man was about to emigrate (usually to America, alas), the tailor would make him a suit and send him on his way, telling him he could pay whenever he returned to Ireland, whether to stay permanently or perhaps just for his mother's funeral. In the same tradition, a general dealer would sponsor shoes and shirts, if need be. The debts were invariably repaid, sometimes five or ten years later. As far as Michael could remember, only the priest, the doctor and the cobbler had no pub into which their visitors might disappear when under stress. How sad that those days are gone.

Not all that far down the road from Tim's estate agency and florists in Lismore, there was a popular public house owned by a taciturn character named Ted Ryan. It was there that we had a half-pint of lager and a cheese sandwich after first meeting Tim the Faithful. The small pub was neatly designed with a small summer garden at the back and an apartment on the floor above the bar which was the home of Ted and his wife. She would generally retire upstairs an hour or two before closing time, leaving him in charge.

Some months after our first meeting, Ted explained to me that a significant proportion of the local population was related, one to the other, either by blood or by marriage. This meant one should choose one's words very carefully when speaking of anyone from the town. This caution did not apply to the same extent when the person under discussion was regarded as a "blow in". Thus Ted felt at liberty to tell me that Tim the Faithful was just such a man, having moved all the way from County Cork (perhaps 75 miles away at the most) to marry a local girl and settle in the town a mere 35 years earlier. He also divulged that Tim had once been an enthusiast for "the creature", otherwise known as Irish whiskey, and could often be seen in town before midday, suitably sedated in a friendly sort of way by a drop or two of the amber liquid.

In the early days, Ted seemed to be a dependable source of information but there was reason to doubt his reliability somewhat later.

His wife, who had gone upstairs when Ted called closing time and had started ushering the last bitter-end guests out, returned unexpectedly 45 minutes later to look for her spectacles. To her considerable indignation, if the gossip was well-founded, she found Ted, the host as he was, extending unusual hospitality to the barmaid, who was allegedly reclining on one of the sturdier wooden tables in the pub. Tears at bedtime. Ted spent the remaining 20 years of his life as a single man.

The circumstances leading to both Tim the Faithful and Michael the Generous becoming total abstainers were explained to me later by one of them, no doubt slightly embellished to amuse me the more.

To this day, the Irish love a really good funeral and even quite poor families do their best to organise a ceremony involving several priests, a decent coffin carried from home to church, songs and eulogies. It is considered a privilege to be invited by the family of the deceased to participate. On a particular day, at least ten years before I met them, Tim and Michael were asked to act as pallbearers at a funeral to be held in a village with which they were unfamiliar, even though it was only some 15 miles away. Good friends as they were, Tim and Michael met in a public house a few hours before the ceremony and refreshed themselves with a few pints of the dark brew whilst discussing their duties, which would include sitting near the coffin during the mass and assisting to carry it out later to the waiting hearse. After a convivial hour or more, now suitably fortified, they repaired to the townland of Ballytree and entered the church on the main street to sit next to each other beside the departed in his handsome oak box. Initially, slightly the worse for wear, they must have both nodded off, rather like members of the British House of Lords after a good luncheon. Tim awoke from his sleep with a start. With admirable clarity of mind, given the circumstances, he now noticed that there was only a single clergyman conducting the service and that he did not appear to be following the usual familiar litany and ritual of a Roman Catholic funeral. Furthermore, when he roused Michael, neither of them could identify a single soul in the congregation. They withdrew from what was a Ballytree Church of Ireland Protestant funeral as quietly as possible and, somewhat unsteadily, made their way across the street to the imposing Catholic edifice nearby, just in time to assist the other pallbearers in bringing the late lamented out to the waiting hearse.

This experience gave both men cause for thought and led directly to their subsequent abstinence. Tim, in particular, became a man of regular and virtuous habits. He attended mass most days of the week and repaired to Ted's bar at lunchtime each day for sandwiches, soup and tea.

Though Tim became a teetotaller, albeit one who frequently pressed a potent Irish-coffee or two on his friends, he continued to consume cigarettes at an alarming rate until well into his late sixties. By that time, he no longer boasted a full set of teeth and the few that remained, stained by nicotine and time, were in a pitiful state, standing askew like the ancient tombstones in a neglected Church of Ireland graveyard.

One morning, I had cause to visit Tim and was taken aback when he smiled, revealing a full set of perfect teeth. Stimulated by some mysterious new insight, or possibly just the fact that he could no longer chew a lamb chop, Tim had had his own few teeth extracted and shining new dentures fitted. He also gave up smoking completely and would tantalize himself by always keeping a sealed pack of cigarettes in his pocket. This he would examine and then discard whenever he felt the urge to smoke.

A man of iron resolve to the end, Tim lived to a great age, finally succumbing to a combination of the inevitable failure of vital functions that awaits all who survive beyond their eighth decade. As people still say here: "God be good to him."

7. NOBLESSE OBLIGE

By the time we became friends, Tim was the main driving force behind most of the charitable work in town and the leader or chairman of a group that planned and collected funds for a splendid new retirement home, replacing an historic stone building that had been something similar to an old English workhouse a century before. The care home was very close to Tim's heart and it became my habit, showing gratitude for the kindness with which my family had been welcomed to Lismore, to pay for the premises to be decorated with flowers from Tim and Rita's shop each Christmas season. This arrangement meant that, in a small way, both the flower shop and the care home would benefit.

Given that the home was in the Republic of Ireland, over ninety percent of the inhabitants were, at least nominally, Roman Catholic. The randy Bishop of Galway and Kilmacduagh, Eamonn Casey, had not yet fallen from grace, and his private life and the various scandals involving that denomination were not yet public knowledge. So the Roman church was still held in high esteem then, at least within the parishes of Lismore and Cappoquin. The aged and conservative Lismore parish priest always admired the beautiful floral arrangements that Rita provided for the care home, particularly those in the hall where he usually said mass for those who were too infirm to attend the church a few blocks distant. Tim took great and impish delight in reminding him that they were the gift of a Protestant, a heretic no less. This information did the priest no obvious harm; he went to his reward at a good age.

Completion of the care home project could not have been realised without the generous support of the English aristocrats who owned a beautiful castle on the banks of the river just outside town. This pile was seen, at least by the duchess, as no more than a small holiday house and indeed, by comparison with the family property in England, it could be regarded as quite modest. It was, however, a beautiful structure in a lovely setting that attracted tourists to the otherwise uninteresting little town.

Members of the noble family and their guests would be in residence there from time to time, and local people were employed both in the castle and its gardens and forests. Famous past guests had included at least one British prime minister, the great dancer Fred Astaire, and also an overweight, bearded King of England who fished in the Blackwater river and was reputed to be not particularly continent, or indeed discriminating, where his choice of lady-friends was concerned. Certainly, at least one of the local Anglo-Irish yeomanry was rumoured to be his direct descendant and therefore, by half measures, a great-uncle to the Queen of England.

The castle was opened regularly for various charitable events and, in later years, was the centre of an opera festival, art exhibitions and smaller events. The family also made land available for a golf course, supported the fabric of some old buildings and rented fishing spots along the river to the general public.

The duke himself was an admirable man with a superb World War II military record that included a Military Cross for bravery when leading his men in Italy. He was, for some time, active in politics and had achieved a great deal preserving and ultimately developing family properties that had been left in dire financial straits by various feckless ancestors. It also should be said, however, that he had a fine reputation for being something of a *bon vivant*, even in his later years.

At a quite advanced age, he attended a charity dinner held in the Athanaeum, a famous and select London club, and found himself seated beside the late Professor Frank Woods CBE, a close friend and colleague of mine and at that time Dean of Medicine at Sheffield University. Once he had established that Frank was a distinguished physician and academic, the noble lord spent the dinner seeking his advice on the merits and possible benefits of always keeping a supply of Viagra close at hand.

There were any number of reports of slightly irregular behaviour on the duke's part, including expensive visits to a house in Park Lane, London, run by a lady of suspect credentials who catered for those needs of impeccable gentlemen that are best met in discreet surroundings. All of these allegations, whether true or not, only served to increase the esteem in which he was held by the citizens of our Deise town. The Irish generally appreciate that bold and eccentric behaviour can add immensely to the gaiety of life and in this, whether intentionally or not, His Grace succeeded. His pardonable offences, as such, were of little interest when weighed against the man's great generosity, impeccable manners and kindness to the ordinary men and women he mixed with in both England and Ireland.

On one occasion, Tim led a small delegation to the castle to meet the duke in a reception room where he would sign a cheque in favour of the planned new care home with an appropriate degree of ceremony. The townsmen were ushered into a room in which a large desk was the most obvious piece of furniture and a few seats had been set out for them. A secretary entered the room, directing the noble lord, who seemed rather flushed and slightly distracted, to the chair behind the desk. Delegates in the front row thought they detected a faint aroma of what was, perhaps, a Midleton single-pot whiskey. A large cheque book was placed in the centre of the desk and a fountain pen handed to the duke. His Grace looked at the pen, muttered something incomprehensible and fell asleep without further ceremony, his forehead on the desk. Quite unflustered, the secretary announced: "His Grace is unable to sign a cheque at present. I shall have it delivered to your office, Mr Hegarty."

A splendid, fearless man, remembered affectionately. He has been quoted as once saying:

Wonderful things have happened in my life – it's time my son had his turn. When I was young I used to like casinos, fast women and God knows what. Now my idea of heaven, apart from being at Chatsworth, is to sit in the hall of Brooks's club having tea.

8. MORE OF THE IRISH

We finally moved into the old Georgian house a mile or two from Lismore in 1991. It was in need of the expert attention of plumbers and electricians, amongst others, but considering how we had spent the first five months of our marriage, Ballinadine was pure luxury. During the first quarter of my internship in a Natal Zulu hospital, we had lived in a roughly converted double garage together with a small white kitten, Florence, who had slept in the chest-of-drawers. She was the first of nearly 20 cats who lived with us during the next 50 years.

A week or so after moving to Ballinadine, we received two visitors, one of whom came over from town quite regularly to make himself comfortable in the living room and chat over a cup of coffee. Pat was the local Garda (police) sergeant and had been detailed to keep an eye on us, given that we were, at that stage, two foreigners. A friendly and personable man, he gave us much useful advice on how best to integrate into our new community. We had, after all, little knowledge of the famine, the Easter Rising or the disgraceful Civil War and the divisions and feuds that followed in its aftermath. The tendency of one particular subsection of the Irish population to celebrate family weddings and funerals by attacking each other with slash-hooks and other agricultural implements was also explained to us from a policing point-of-view. We were invited to call upon him for advice and assistance at any time. These friendly visits were a disorienting experience for people who had spent the first 45 years of their lives in Nationalist South Africa, being more than slightly uncomfortable in the presence of policemen and, more especially, special branch (security) officers.

The second visitor was a parish priest from the village five miles to our east. Father Michael was keen to draw us into the arms of his very active Roman Catholic congregation. A warm and genial individual, he accepted the offer of a glass of Jamieson's whiskey from my wife with the speed a sprinter at the start of the Olympic 100 meters race might well envy. Either from native courtesy or else in consequence of the well-known, pleasing medicinal effects of this refreshment, Father Michael spoke well of us. He remarked that he could detect clear signs of residual decency in both of us even though it had been confessed to him, with some embarrassment, that we were actually Protestants, some of whose Irish forebears might have been good Catholics before the famine. "You are two of our own," he said.

A first-rate man, the reverend father was next heard from when he became involved in an ultimately successful attempt to close the popular bordello that operated in a pink house, conveniently situated midway between his village church and a local pharmacy. There is no record of how many parishioners chose obedience to the rules of chastity above the attractions of the pink house but, no doubt, the pharmacy had a slightly increased turnover during this interlude. In any event, it seems likely that Father Michael became depressed by frequent calls upon his time to attend the confessional and deal with numbers of almost certainly unrepentant members of his congregation seeking absolution. Whatever his real thoughts were on this issue cannot possibly be said, but his work with the otherwise holy patrons of the pink house must have drained his resources, psychologically if not physically. He retired from the parish soon afterwards, claiming ill-health due to high blood pressure, and moved to a care home for the devout somewhere on the southern coast of Ireland. There he perished peacefully in due course.

Our house in Ireland had belonged to a German non-resident who had invested money in several properties in the area of West Waterford. From him we inherited a small family that lived in the gatehouse cottage and a gardener of mature years. He was someone who, by his charm and relaxed nature, provided us with some early insights into the way of life in rural Ireland at that time.

Michael, called Mick by us to distinguish him from all the other local Michaels, was a small man who believed, quite rightly, in doing everything at his own pace. He was in his seventh or eighth decade when first we met, a short, stocky, pinkish man with a pleasant, open face. He wore horn-rimmed spectacles and was balding with a few wisps of nondescript hair on the crown of his head that became unruly in a random way when the wind blew. At work, he usually wore old-fashioned dungarees and was given to using gardening tools of a traditional nature, as if he were Mr McGregor in a Beatrix Potter story, rather than any more modern, labour-saving devices. Ordinary hedge-clippers or a scythe were more to his liking than, say, a petrol-driven strimmer, and simple tools suited the steady, even leisurely, pace at which he laboured. There were two elderly donkeys and an old cart in the paddock near the main house and the general impression was that, of all his duties, Mick's favourite pastime was to hitch the younger of the two asses to the cart and go around the acres of garden in this way, collecting leaves and cut grass for composting. So now and then we would come home of an autumn afternoon to behold a scene, in our own garden, that would have gladdened the heart of the famous English painter, Constable.

Coming from Africa, we were accustomed to employing a gardener who, through no fault of his own, was very poorly educated and might well be illiterate. Communication would be by way of a mixture of broken English and Zulu. The meaning of life or the ethics of value added taxes would not come up for discussion as a rule. We soon learnt that our Irish friend was a different proposition altogether.

For a start, Mick arrived at work in a small but functional motor car and, during his lunchbreak, would sit in the car eating sandwiches provided by the sister with whom he lived and reading a newspaper that was spread open and balanced on the steering wheel before him. The newspaper was always a broadsheet. That is to say, it was never one of the best-selling newspapers designed for the entertainment of those semi-literate adults that have little interest in text and simply look at images, paying special attention to those depicting footballers and perfectly-formed young women.

In due course it was explained to us, by Mick himself, that he was a keen follower of horse-racing. Like the esteemed Tim Hegarty, he had the habit of scanning the racing pages daily for advice on which trainer, jockey or horses to back. Most of the time, one suspects, this would be a difficult task since race meetings were so frequent in Ireland. Presumably there were at least as many florid characters involved in Irish racing then as in any Damon Runyon tales of Regret the Horseplayer and Hot Horse Herbie. There was never talk of either Tim or Mick losing much on the turf. Perhaps they bore in mind one of Runyon's famous pieces of advice:

The race is not always to the swift nor the battle to the strong,
but that's the way to bet.

His racing knowledge apart, we had good reason to be impressed by Michael's way with words. One often hears that the Irish can charm the birds from the trees but how often would someone in England have his gardener in muddy Wellington boots come over to him and say, "Doctor, sure herself has found the keys she accused you of losing. So now you are entirely exonerated."? A few such exchanges taught the "blow-ins", as newcomers are called for their first 30 or 40 years in Ireland, never to underestimate the natives.

Inevitably Michael began to slow down during the ten years after our arrival although he only blotted his copybook once in that time. Whilst preoccupied, perhaps thinking of a likely winner at the Galway Races, he cleared the library hearth and deposited the still hot coals in the woodshed. Even now the walls bear witness to the fire that resulted but it was extinguished easily enough. After a while he retired, lived for a few seasons with his widowed sister and then ended his days in a care home. A gentle, kindly fellow who belonged in the 1950s, made no fuss, and who harmed nobody.

9. THE POACHER

One of the best men that I ever came across in Ireland, or elsewhere for that matter, was my neighbour, Michael the Poacher. A fine looking man in his prime, he lived perhaps 200 paces from my front door down a quiet boreen. An ex-soldier, who had served with Irish peace-keeping forces in the Middle East, Michael became friendly after he had observed me "giving out" about some activities of the generally splendid duke who sometimes resided in the local castle.

At the top of my property there was an orchard that was enclosed by high stone walls, presumably built in the days of the Irish famine. This abutted onto a plantation belonging to the duke, whose men would harvest trees there from time to time and put the wood to good purpose. Immediately above the wall was a row of about eight beautiful old Scots pines which were part of the territory occupied by a family of rare, indeed endangered, red squirrels that were a picture to see on a sunny day. On just such a day, I was startled to hear the sound of chainsaws near the house and, on investigation, discovered that a group of four local men had set about felling the firs.

One of the men was Michael. When I questioned them, they told me that they were taking down the trees as directed by the duke's manager, in order to widen the path along which they proposed to drive tractors deeper into the plantation to fell and collect mature trees. My response was, in the first place, to turn a nasty shade of purple and to ask if they could not find a better way to spend their time than working for a "bloody Englishman". As it turned out, the tree-felling exercise was illegal and the police and forestry commission became involved, though not in time to save more than one of these magnificent trees. The squirrels moved house and I still meet their descendants from time to time in my lower garden area.

I made an abject apology to the men later on the same day. After all, the level of unemployment was high at the time and the duke's manager could just as well have brought in willing workers from elsewhere. The locals were simply taking advantage of an opportunity to work and earn wages near their own homes and, in the process, keep food on their tables. My remarks to them had been quite out of order and uncalled for – shameful, actually, even if the Irishmen secretly approved of the sentiments.

Later that week, an assistant manager, a most charming Anglo-Irish fellow, came to my door to explain in very civil terms that what happened on the duke's property was, essentially, none of my business. That might have been fair comment had one of the trees belonging to His Grace not fallen on and damaged, though not demolished, one of my stone walls. My reply was to the point, namely: "You English are no more than a bunch of vandals." A bit unfair unless one is speaking of football hooligans. He received this news with aplomb, remarking that he was sorry to hear that such was my opinion. At the time, I was unaware that this quiet, almost apologetic, man had been decorated for bravery during the Troubles in Ulster and that his wider family could boast an impressive number of awards for exceptional courage, including a Zulu War Victoria Cross, a VC and Bar in the Great War and several Military Crosses. Later, a local wit told me that my visitor might well have been decorated for personally carrying a live terrorist explosive device out of an occupied building, but that this only proved how unsuited he was to be serving in the British army intelligence corps. In due course, we attended the same church, both wore the poppy in November, and became on friendly terms. An admirable man with bravery in his blood. He was pleased, as our relationship developed, to learn from me that the terms "bloody", "buggers" and "bastards" as applied to people of any nationality by South Africans in casual conversation carried roughly the same weight as the terms "chaps" or "fellows" did when uttered by an Englishman. This nomenclature never caught on in the Deise, however, where men still refer to one another as "feckers".

Michael the Poacher did not believe in showing deference to British aristocrats or their agents, and so my ill-tempered behaviour, which he witnessed that day, cheered him up immensely. His own resistance to the old enemy took a different form and lasted for years. He was a devout believer in the health-giving properties of fresh fish and so was an inveterate and successful poacher of the duke's riverine domain.

One of the strangest aspects of life in Ireland, at least to me, was that a number of laws, promulgated by the English crown many centuries before, remained on the statute books of the Irish Republic. Thus, lands stolen by various monarchs or by Oliver Cromwell were distributed amongst their sycophants and soldiers, some staying in the hands of such men's descendants to the present day. In this odd way, a major sector of the Blackwater was ceded to the duke and his descendants from surface to river bottom. Licences were required to fish these waters.

In common with most rational republicans, Michael was unimpressed by this absurd ruling and would spend many a clear, dark night poaching salmon and grils along the Deise stretch of the river. Following the altercation over the Scots pines, we became regular beneficiaries of his sorties down to the Blackwater. He would arrive at the front door bearing a fine fish which he would present with the words: "Here's one that the fecking duke will never get to cook."

When Michael had word that my wife, Pat, was dying and had only a week or two to live, he brought me two beautiful brown trout, taken from the river before sunrise, together with his wife's advice that they be cooked in butter. The fish proved to be tender and delicious and were eaten with relish by the patient who, understandably enough, had a very poor appetite at the time. If a bottle of New Zealand Sauvignon Blanc was not opened at the time, it should have been.

Perhaps ten days later, as is customary in Ireland, friends showed their respect for Pat by visiting her, lying in a closed casket at the local funeral home, on the day before her funeral. Family members stood beside the coffin to greet the visitors and respond to their words of comfort. The sad event was attended by both Catholic and Protestant clergy, an unusual compliment to the departed and evidence of the innate kindness, compassion and decency of the Irish people at large.

Michael came along, accompanied by his wife, and shook my hand with the firmest of grips. "I am sorry for your troubles," he said. "But at least she had the trout." Heartfelt sentiments indeed and from a man amongst men.

Sadly, poor Michael had his own unexpected appointment in Samara only a few years later. He was killed instantly by a tree that fell unexpectedly whilst he was, as so often in the past, one of a group of workers in one of the duke's plantations. Perhaps if he had taken to heart my uncouth comments about working for the English, he might yet be alive.

How fortunate to have once known such a man. As the saying goes, "He did what it says on the tin." His way of life was in complete contrast to the brave new era that so often champions the unhappy viewpoints of dysfunctional "experts" and even, at times, of known pathological liars.

10. EXILES

As time passes, it becomes increasingly difficult to differentiate between those interesting people one actually met, and once knew quite well, and others of whom one had only heard stories or even, perhaps, only dreamt. To make matters worse, as noted by Elizabeth II, some recollections are more accurate than others.

During the 1950s and 1960s, my teachers and older relatives would occasionally make dark references concerning people they identified as "remittance men". As in: "That fellow Fotherington is a remittance man, you know."

It transpired that these were individuals, almost always men, who had been an embarrassment to their (often prominent) families in England and had been outlawed and despatched "abroad", there to remain in exile. In exchange for an undertaking never to return home, these naughty men were removed to Europe, Ireland or some far-flung colonial country where they lived and were supported, often in some style, by regular cash remittances from their parents or other relatives in England. The background of these interesting individuals would naturally be the subject of gossip and speculation. In at least one famous example from years gone by, a remittance man, who settled in a South African village in an area known as the Garden Route, was rumoured to be the illegitimate offspring of an English king. The rumour was supported to an extent by what was known of the monarch's careless habits and by the man's physical appearance and name: George Rex.

None of the men who were pointed out to me as being members of this category were quite as interesting as Mr Rex. Most seemed to be idle, if not altogether feckless, and had presumably been invited to leave the polite family circles from which they came because of persistent gauche behaviour in public. At least one of them, however, did give rise to a certain amount of hilarity and mirth amongst the country set in Tipperary.

When I met him, the Honourable Cuthbert St Étienne Dewsbury was in late middle-age, or so it seemed. His alcohol intake was, after all, such that he might well have been much older physically than he actually was chronologically. He was known to spend time in various rural pubs with the famous Dr Daley, who had befriended him initially in the belief that Dewsbury, being of noble provenance, would have funds from which he might readily be separated.

Whatever his income, the Hon Cuthbert was, at the very least, an entertaining fellow. His bizarre public schoolboy accent alone was worth listening to, and he seemed to have come from an interesting enough background at the upper end of the English social scale. Of course, once he got beyond explaining the old school tie that he regularly sported beneath his frayed collars, it became increasingly difficult to decide whether what he had to say was factual or not. In part this was thanks to the degree to which his alcohol intake interfered with the clarity of his speech. Amongst other tales, he was fond of telling anyone who would listen that amongst his forbears were French aristocrats and hence the reference to St Étienne in his baptismal name. He claimed that, as a small boy, his great-great-grandfather had been hidden in a Parisian chimney by servants whilst the rest of the family were taken away for guillotining by the charming and humane 18th century revolutionaries of that place.

The Honourable Cuthbert Dewsbury really hated the Irish habit of addressing everyone by their Christian names. He found this relaxed, friendly approach very annoying and patronising, and eventually took action to block it. All things considered, he found it unreasonable that, without any formal introduction, he should be called Cuthbert when members of the clergy, of whom he heartily disapproved, expected to be addressed with due deference by their title: Father or Bishop, perhaps, but certainly not Frank, Mick or Pat. When he was admitted to hospital so that his inguinal hernia could be attended to, he informed the staff that his first name was "Cyr", pronounced "Sir" – quite witty and understandable, perhaps. How many upper-class Brits of mature years, sporting an old Harrovian tie, would be happy to have some callow young Irish nurse say: "Have your bowels moved today at all, Cuthbert?" Rather let it be: "Please take your pill now, Sir."

After a while the drinking habits of the Hon Cuthbert Dewsbury led to absences from human company and reality, and he would withdraw from a party or bar either silently and without comment or else after saying to the other inebriates that he was going home. He would usually be reported to the guardians of the peace as missing at 3 or 4a.m. by his anxious, long-suffering housekeeper, the widowed Mrs Brigid O'Reilly. As a rule, they found the Honourable Cuthbert within an hour or two, sleeping soundly in his car. This might be parked on the roadside or in a ditch, somewhere along the route from his host's place to his own home. He succumbed, in time, to the toxic effects of over-indulgence in his favourite form of gargle and joined his ancestors, French or British as they might have been.

Not just remittance men were obliged to keep their distance from England. Some individuals were "persons of interest" to the British constabulary for one reason or another. Now and then, a senior Irish politician would manage to have charges withdrawn against a friend or relative who had misbehaved on the larger island by giving a solemn undertaking to stop him from ever visiting Britain again: a civilized arrangement well before the horrors of investigative journalism and one that probably worked to everyone's satisfaction. Usually, the miscreants who were dealt with in this way were little more than fairly harmless serial offenders with a recurrent impulse to shoplift, use public transport without a ticket or to indulge in what used to be referred to, rather primly, as "insulting behaviour in public".

In a case of which I was aware, the guilty party was a man with inherited wealth and a rumoured connection, through his somewhat flighty grandmother, with European royalty. A monarch of generous proportions used to visit Ireland, part of his kingdom at that time, mainly to hunt and to kill salmon which were plentiful in the Blackwater. By most accounts, he was surprisingly agile in spite of his bulk and was known to have the libido of a prize stallion. In any event, he left his imprint here and there.

Simon Milligan, the alleged grandson of His Majesty, and himself the father of a large family, had two passions over and above regularly wasting handy sums of money at the Galway Races. One of these was trout fishing all over the British Isles. The other was walking from his London club in St James to Green Park where he would entertain himself by committing a public order offence that was both annoying and insulting to those who walked by. His *modus operandi* would be to hide behind one of the many trees that line the paths there and leap out, exposing his impolite parts to astonished ladies who might be strolling by, whether alone or walking their dogs. In due course, he was apprehended.

Milligan was thought to be a basically harmless fellow who probably would not have hurt a fly but, even so, could not be allowed to continue indulging himself indefinitely in "insulting behaviour" without sanction. After several warnings had been issued, and by agreement with an Irish cabinet minister who intervened on his behalf, he resigned from his club in London and was debarred from England and Wales. He was allowed still to visit the Scottish highlands to catch trout. This much appreciated exemption was presumably granted because the Metropolitan Police Chief was himself a devotee of fly-fishing, if not flashing, and understood how much pain exclusion from the river bank would cause the well-connected Mr Milligan.

An eclectic group of individuals across the western world, almost invariably men, have evidently made a habit of this curious behaviour. Amongst others, there was a member of the South African cabinet who retired quietly after he was seen on several occasions exposing himself to the nightly Johannesburg to Durban express train as it passed at speed through the centre of his Natal constituency at about three in the morning. Flashing is no longer regarded as either funny or entirely harmless. It seems that what was once the practice of essentially bewildered and rather pathetic little men has spread to a more dangerous selection of individuals associated with serious crimes against women. So we are told.

11. CHANCERS

There have most certainly been beggars, thieves, pickpockets and imaginative fraudsters for millennia. The non-violent amongst them have been working their way through the naïve, the elderly and the kind-hearted since long before the internet and the smartphone were invented. Obviously, the unwary are easily fooled when a plausible story is invented by a clever scam-artist. Of late, any number of heartrending stories with requests for financial assistance have appeared on media platforms, usually in the middle of discussions of a totally unconnected subject, such as a sporting event, celebrity concert or even the announcement of a family birthday or marriage. Most people have had some contact with these sociable petty criminals, some of whose approaches can be quite inventive and, looked at objectively from a safe distance, comical. In Ireland, there is a portmanteau word used to describe people in this category. They are referred to as "chancers".

In the heyday of the Catholic Church in Ireland, which probably ended before the turn of the present century, priests enjoyed a period when they were treated with great deference by most people in the country to the extent that their motives and activities away from the altar were hardly ever questioned. It should therefore be no surprise to learn that more than one middle-aged confidence trickster in Munster was able to earn a useful steady income by dressing himself as a priest and collecting donations (for black babies in the Congo or orphans with hare-lips in Brazil) in areas remote from the public houses where he was best known. He was, almost certainly, not the only *faux* priest in circulation.

Some fraudsters checked their references really well, and one with whom I was acquainted was amongst those who believed in being diligent in that regard. The Reverend Patrick Mooney, after purchasing a degree in divinity for US $250 via the website of a no-questions-asked virtual university based in Wyoming, set about his career across the length and breadth of Ireland. He was a small, rather well-rounded but neat and dignified looking fellow of about 60 summers and was, as seems essential for those that make a career of deception, well-spoken and gifted with a gravity of manner that made his pose quite convincing. His activities in the Blackwater Valley were relatively limited but illustrated the intelligence with which he operated. They were also sufficiently successful to provide for his essential requirements during a slack period of a few weeks whilst he was planning his next move.

The irreverent gentleman read in the local papers that the dean of the Anglican cathedral had died and would not be replaced for at least eight weeks. His replacement needed time to wind up affairs in the Mayo parish where he occupied a very busy living as vicar to a large congregation. Patrick Mooney put the information to good use and after adjusting the colour of the bib beneath his home-made clerical collar, passed himself off in the mostly Roman Catholic community as the new Protestant dean. For almost two months, he kept his car filled with petrol and his larder and wine cellar stocked with quality items purchased "on account". As invariably seems to happen, he disappeared without trace once he felt that the game would soon be up and well before the relaxed rural police began to show any interest in him. A talented thespian, really.

Several of us bumped into the would-be dean but any contact with Dinny the Spy, if indeed he ever existed, would have been limited to members of our parents' generation.

Terrible things happened in Ireland during the first quarter of the 20th century. About 40,000 young men died during World War I, and patriots, soldiers and innocent bystanders died during the Easter Rising, the War of Independence and the awful Civil War of 1922 to 1923. In consequence, the question of whether Ireland should take up arms against Hitler in 1939 was divisive and the country remained neutral, though tilted slightly in favour of assisting British forces in which many men and women of Irish origin served.

One man who was happy to be of service to the Allies, for a small fee of course, was one Daniel "Dinny" O'Sullivan, a native of Dingle on the Kerry coast. He had been supplied with a telescope and was asked to report on any sightings of suspicious shipping in the area, with particular emphasis upon German U-boats. His handler, Hamilton Blunden, a large, bibulous Englishman with a handle-bar moustache and expensively earned red nose, would come across from Killarney, where his radio contact with the Admiralty was situated, and meet O'Sullivan quite regularly. On one occasion, Blunden (Harrow, Grenadier Guards, major, retired) was unable to travel to Dingle due to a severe attack of gout. He sent his wireless operator, Oswald J. Ferguson, to meet O'Sullivan instead.

Ferguson was instructed to find Daniel "Dinny" O'Sullivan in Dingle and to identify himself as a *bona fide* contact by means of an agreed code. Dinny would be at ease on hearing him say: "Sure it will be a sad day for Ireland if ever we lose the Galway Races." They could then safely exchange useful information regarding the local maritime movements of the wicked and devious Hun. Dinny, for his part, would provide just enough fictitious information to keep the agents of King George interested.

This took place in 1943, well before the James Bond era, but one imagines Ferguson knew *The Thirty-nine Steps* and the Bulldog Drummond adventure stories. So he set off for Dingle, delighted to be a fully-fledged espionage agent. Visions of a future investiture at Buckingham Palace crossed his mind and he wondered if his visiting cards would soon read "Sir Oswald Ferguson Kt." .

When he arrived in Dingle town at about four in the afternoon, he realised all might not be plain sailing. For a start, there was abundant evidence that the name O'Sullivan was an extremely common one in that parish. The largest public house, a hardware shop and a grocery store all had the name D. O'Sullivan inscribed on the window or front door.

A resourceful man, Oswald Ferguson, who was convinced he knew the Irish form, decided to start his search in the pub and then go on to the stores if he had no luck amongst the drinkers. He entered the hostelry to find a group of five hearty looking men nursing glasses of dark stout at the bar. "Excuse me," he said, after ordering a lemonade for himself. "Would any of you gentlemen be Mr O'Sullivan by any chance?" Three of the five raised a free hand and the barman looked interested. "I need to speak to Dinny O'Sullivan on a confidential matter." The host put down the beer glass he was polishing, leaned over the bar and, addressing Ferguson, said: "By all means and why not, you are very welcome. I am Dinny O'Sullivan myself."

Oswald J. Ferguson was delighted to have made contact so easily and so quickly. Taking the barman aside, a few paces away from the counter and the stout drinkers, he whispered: "Sure it will be a sad day for Ireland if ever we lose the Galway races." "Jaysus, indeed, yes," said O'Sullivan and then, turning to address his customers, said, "Himself is looking for Dinny the Spy. Does any of youse know where he is at all?"

Security was not all that tight in Ireland, one suspects.

12. A DROP OF THE HARD STUFF

Tradition would have it that the Irish are seriously committed heavy drinkers and are almost always ready for a fight once liquor has been taken. That description certainly holds good for a small proportion of Irishmen, particularly so, it would seem, amongst those who have not lived in their home country for years and are a good remove away in England or, worse still, America. The truth is that in Ireland itself a quite large percentage of both men and women do not drink at all. Those who do take alcohol tend to be quite civilized in their ways and to follow a regular pattern of sorts when in the pubs that they usually patronise. The intake might or might not result in the drinker becoming marginally euphoric now and then or even, in extreme cases, immobilised but, in general, decorum is preserved.

A typical example of what might be termed quiet and unobtrusive drinking was given by one of my neighbours, a man who, in his time, was almost an icon in the local village. Mickey-Joe McCarthy, known to one and all as Little Mick the Oracle, was a man in his late sixties who appreciated an occasional drop of what that Presbyterian hero, the Reverend Ian Paisley, used to call The Devil's Buttermilk. His preference, however, was not for whiskey but to sit at a bar counter for hours, late morning and evening, in his tired-looking hacking-jacket and corduroys, gradually working his way through no more than a few pints of stout. He would walk the mile and a half to and from his farmer's cottage to town twice almost every day.

Normally a quiet, even introverted fellow, Mickey-Joe would begin his daily vigils silently, gazing rather sadly at the brown liquid in his glass. As time passed, he would become ever more affable and strike up conversations with any audience, even one that was made up of blow-ins and strangers from abroad. He had quite definite views on a wide range of subjects and was happy to share them with one and all, particularly those generous enough to fill his glass. There is no record of whether anyone ever really noticed that his comments became progressively more irrational, and indeed slurred, as the fifth, sixth and seventh pints were taken. Presumably some of his companions were keeping pace with his intake themselves and therefore it can be imagined that they followed his logic perfectly and that, to them, his words had all the weight and wisdom of an Aristotle or a Plato. An Oracle indeed.

What is well-known, however, and is a credit to the benign and charitable nature of the Irish, is that Mickey-Joe would frequently need to be taken home in the landlord's car towards the end of the day. This course of action was taken either because Mick had been found fast asleep in the lavatories or, becoming more tired and emotional than usual, had fallen off his bar-stool in the strangely relaxed manner of those whose blood-alcohol levels are particularly high.

There is no doubt that the few irresponsible individuals that drink and drive their cars are a cause of great trouble in most western countries. They are no joke and deserve to be utterly condemned. Now and then, however, drunken antics do raise a smile in spite of the dangers, to self and innocent bystanders, that are inherent in being incoherent, unsteady and uncoordinated.

A few years ago, at about six in the morning, a little boat was seen sailing erratically along a Dublin harbour quay, in the process of endangering traffic in a shipping lane that led out to the open sea. A cruise ship of 4000 tonnes was unable to enter the harbour on schedule because of the danger presented by this small craft. Two men were seen to be aboard, drinking freely from a number of glass bottles. They later claimed in court that these bottles contained nothing more potent than water and that the green colour of the glass was simply an indication that the bottles were "of foreign origin".

Attempts by port authorities and the life-boat service to bring the lively crew and boat to safe moorings proved fruitless and, as a final option, the Gardai (police) were summoned. When they came alongside in their own craft, the "captain" of the unruly boat advised the Garda in charge that he had "a God-given right to sail where I please" and allegedly suggested, in abusive and very basic Anglo-Saxon terms, that the police should go elsewhere. The men in blue managed to hide their amusement and manoeuvred the boat to the quay where the "captain" and his incoherent one-man crew were placed under arrest.

Whether the two were as intoxicated as the press reports suggested is difficult to confirm, since the Gardai were so bewildered by the unusual nature of these events that they forgot to breathalyse their prisoners. It was recorded, however, that the crewman seemed barely able to walk and had to be assisted to step from the boat onto the quayside. This deficit, he later claimed, was not because he was manifestly uncoordinated due to drink taken but because he was arthritic.

When he reached dry land, the same crewman immediately took off all of his clothes and stood naked at the waterside, a scene that was photographed and circulated by news media. From the image published, one might deduce that it was a very cold morning indeed.

Irishmen are seldom at a loss for unlikely explanations, it seems. When our nude crewman came to court a couple of years afterwards, he told the judge that he had disrobed because he feared the gardai, some of whom were armed, might shoot him. If that seems like an irrational piece of thinking on his part, it might be justified by accepting that on the day in question he was not at his best, it being so early an hour of the morning.

The charges faced by the two sailors included careless, drunk sailing and a breach of the peace under Maritime Law. The judge somehow managed to keep a straight face whilst listening to the evidence presented and, deciding in favour of the prosecution, ruled that the accused had indeed been reckless in their behaviour. They had also failed to show any signs of remorse and remained defiant in their claim that they had been within their rights to sail anywhere that they damned well pleased.

The boat was destroyed and captain and crew each given a short custodial sentence. In addition, a hefty fine was imposed and the men were instructed to enrol on an alcohol awareness programme. Permission to appeal was granted.

Recently the case against the captain was dismissed and one hopes the "crew" will also be exonerated. Surely, but for the marine safety question, no harm was done and the antics of the sailors, alleged or not, amused almost everyone.

13. FACTS OF LIFE

Shortly after the violence that attended World War I, the struggle for Irish independence and the bloody civil war, Ireland, with the connivance of unlovely politicians, had become dominated to an unhealthy extent by the diktats of the Church of Rome. *Inter alia,* social contact between the young of opposite sexes was strictly controlled, and Gabriel's bedroom, described in Pardonable Offences, would most certainly not have sheltered so much as a single French letter had the Spikins lived in Ireland. In fact, for a while it was debated whether police should have the power to search citizens, at random, for contraceptives. Extraordinary! Basically, sex was hardly ever mentioned except as a duty that married couples might perform of a Saturday with reproduction, not pleasure, in mind.

Naturally enough, and perhaps to the outrage of the Archbishop of Dublin, that simple holy agenda never received unanimous support within Ireland and, relatively discreetly, the time-honoured mating rituals of the careless young were followed in spite of anything the church and its adherents might have to say. Places intended for other pursuits such as rooms in office blocks, hotels, public houses, restaurants, colleges and even churches were put to good use. In Margaret's case, as with many young women of the time, no overtly romantic ritual would accompany her loss of innocence when it did, in due course, occur. Nothing more complicated than curiosity on her part and a bout of keenly felt lust on that of her debaucher attended her introduction to the unchaste world of adult entertainments.

At Margaret's Dublin convent, in keeping with the strict rulings of the archbishop, no lessons in human sexuality were included in the curriculum taught by the Sisters of Mercy. It seems most unlikely that any of the nuns would have been able to provide their pupils with useful theoretical or practical knowledge on such matters anyway, whatever impression the Decameron Nights might have given regarding the secret recreations of nuns, priests, bishops or monks. So, the subject of human reproduction was carefully avoided by the contemporary Irish Roman Catholic Church, at least when it came to the education of girls in their early teens. It would be heathen protestants, such as the Methodists down the road, who taught pupils "the facts of life". No doubt, in the envious eyes of the nuns, this encouraged them shamelessly to enjoy themselves in all kinds of delightful and forbidden ways that were rightly closed to the obedient followers of Rome.

Lessons at the convent stressed social graces, the importance of regularly attending mass, supporting the church financially, deferring to the priests and nuns at all times, and avoiding heresy and the sins of the flesh. Precise details of how, where and when one might have an opportunity to avoid or even go so far as to commit these last-mentioned sins were not easy to come by. It was well known, however, that actual enjoyment of such activities would turn an already grave mortal sin into an even greater abomination. Indeed, some of the more religious let it be known that merely thinking of fornication might bring you to the very gates of hell. It is encouraging to reflect that such inhuman teachings did nothing to reduce the impudent curiosity of healthy young girls.

Disapproval of matters concerning interplay between the sexes was not limited to the clergy, it should be said. Mothers also avoided discussing intimate matters with their daughters beyond, perhaps, warning them not to wash their hair or sit on the crossbar of a boy's bicycle during a certain phase of the moon, when such bold acts would apparently have dire and unmentionable consequences. Later, most of the girls discovered that shampooing their hair was a pretty harmless activity if you kept soap from your eyes and that it was not the rigidity of a bicycle crossbar that was most likely to get them into trouble with boys.

So, intrigued or not, the pre-pubertal girls concentrated on their school lessons. They were distracted occasionally by playground conversations with the bolder 13 and 14 year olds, who shared what little knowledge they had of adult games with one another and compared notes as the early signs of womanhood began to appear. Famously unreliable sources of information such as popular films and suspect novels were subject to strict censorship by the priesthood of the period and so what was much later to be called "fake news" circulated amongst the young instead. Rumours were abroad that lovers could bring untold (but definitely forbidden) pleasure to one another by what was referred to as "doing it". The girls did not really understand what "it" was, though bold and deliciously wicked acts involving nakedness and peculiar physical activities were spoken of. Naturally, with an almost complete lack of reliable information, and no social contact with the opposite sex other than under the baleful supervision of the supposedly celibate nuns and priests, curiosity ultimately got the better of most of the convent pupils as they entered their late teens.

Margaret had two slightly unsettling experiences whilst still at school. Once, on her way home, a rather shabby-looking individual in a fawn raincoat appeared unexpectedly from behind a garden wall with his flies open, and proudly made a shattering announcement. "This is called a prick", he said. An accurate enough observation on his part, though, for the sake of clarity, he might well have added that it was a small example of its kind. Margaret turned and made off so swiftly that she had no more than a fleeting glimpse of the man's exhibit. Just for a second, as she ran away, she wondered if she should go back and ask him to repeat his presentation so that she might become *au fait* with exactly what "a prick" looked like, if only for future reference. As it was, caution won the day.

Her only other experience of this kind was not much more instructive. On the second occasion, Margaret noticed a medium-sized blue car, parked near to the school gates. A balding man of about her father's age, dressed in city clothes, was seated behind the steering-wheel. At first, some twenty paces distant, she thought that the man was talking to himself but then realised he was calling her to come over to his car. As she approached, Margaret could see that he was grinning and looking down at something in his lap that he seemed to be polishing with considerable vigour, bringing his left arm and hand to bear. Worried and thinking his behaviour odd, she turned her back on him and went home. So, she remained unenlightened.

The frustrated flasher, presumably, lived to fight, or at least expose himself, another day.

Margaret left school to train as a typist and found work after her seventeenth birthday in the office of Plunket, Dunne and Noonan Limited, a legal firm near to her home. By then, she still had no boyfriends. At work, surrounded by older women, Margaret felt callow and, in fact, slightly embarrassed by her state of almost total ignorance. She shared a large desk with a friendly, relatively sophisticated, young woman named Peggy Murray who helped her to settle into the daily routine. They were both answerable to a manager by the name of Patrick Noonan, who had his own office in the cellar of the nineteenth century building in which the company was housed.

Mr Noonan was easy enough to work for and, though he believed himself to be very attractive to women, fell short of being good-looking by several yards. At 43, he was swarthy with brooding, saturnine looks, dark eyes and a sallow skin, made more evident by the white shirts he wore with his creased blue or grey, off-the-peg suits. His general appearance, similar to that of Mr Stromboli, the villain of the piece in Walt Disney's *Pinocchio*, was not improved by the fact that he was a chain-smoker. His jacket, shirt and tie were all liberally decorated with spilt ash. To add to this less than attractive and seductive picture, his teeth and fingers were stained a yellowish-orange colour by nicotine and his clothing always had about as much fragrance as a public house before the ashtrays are emptied or windows opened in the morning. Usually friendly, he could at times be slightly morose. This was attributed by the younger members of staff to the fact that his wife, who occasionally delivered his sandwiches to the office, was a large, imposing and possibly discipline-enforcing woman. Her girth was considered to be quite impressive, even exceptional, in 1959 but would be unremarkable in the present century when women resembling mobile barrels of lard have become commonplace and to comment upon any undesirable aspect of morbid obesity is regarded as "hate speech". No doubt Maeve Noonan had many fine, if less than obvious, virtues. A neat handwriting, a kind heart or an ability to provide a full Irish breakfast at short notice, perhaps.

Whatever cross Mr Noonan had to bear, he did seem to find some consolation in taking a very personal interest in his staff, particularly Peggy Murray. That this could be described as a hands-on approach became evident to Margaret soon after she began working for Plunket, Dunne and Noonan.

Peggy, a pretty girl of about 25, would be summoned to Mr Noonan's office from time to time, ostensibly to take dictation. Margaret noticed that she often returned to her desk from these visits to the basement more than somewhat less poised and elegant than before. A little flustered, her normally neat hair slightly unruly, her cheeks ruddy, lipstick smudged and, now and then, a stocking laddered or a seam off-centre. It seemed that either she made a habit of falling downstairs on the way to or from his office in the cellar or else that Mr Noonan had involved her in some sort of aerobic activity that was more testing than simply dictating letters or lighting cigarettes. Irish dancing perhaps?

At first, it did not occur to Margaret that more than just ash might be spilled in Mr Noonan's office or that he could well be just the man to come to her rescue and put an end to her wretched virginal status. Later, the penny dropped, even though she had never asked Peggy about her visits downstairs.

One day, after Margaret had been employed for about a year, Mr Noonan called her to his office on some pretext and asked, without preamble, if she would care to accompany him later that day on a brief visit to the mountains just beyond the city. The fact that he grinned at her in a wolfish manner as he said this made it clear enough, even to an innocent, that what he had in mind was not for her to go with him on an expedition to chase butterflies, pick sprigs of heather or watch the starlings gathering at dusk.

She accepted his invitation.

14. MR NOONAN DISAPPOINTS

To Margaret Hogan, Mr Noonan's invitation was a clear signal that her day of deliverance had finally arrived, albeit somewhat unexpectedly. It was arranged that she would wait at the end of a nearby street immediately after work and he would collect her there in his car, a slightly worse-for-wear Morris Oxford. It was what passed for summer in that part of the world, with long bright evenings but not that much warmth. So Margaret wore a coat over her floral frock, beneath which the usual feminine undergarments were, of course, in place. As it was a Friday, she also wore her best leather shoes: high-heeled, pointed and tomato red, a fashionable colour amongst young women of the day as were bright green and yellow.

The interior of the small two-door car was foggy with cigarette smoke by the time Mr Noonan arrived at their meeting place and he smoked throughout the drive along narrow roads into the hills south of Dublin and in the direction of Wicklow. Not a word was spoken. Mr Noonan did not discuss what they would do once they arrived at their destination and, since nothing was said, must have simply taken it for granted, rather like an early version of Mr Harvey Weinstein, that Margaret knew and gave her full, if uninformed, consent to whatsoever he planned. In this, leaving aside her almost complete ignorance of such activities, he was actually correct. Impatient to lose her innocence, she sat quietly beside him, excitedly anticipating the delights she had been told to expect.

As a good girl, educated by nuns, Margaret had no idea whether any special etiquette should be adhered to by a young woman either before during or after her introduction to carnal pleasures by a worldly, adept, older man.

On the road, she did wonder if any special protocols were followed in such circumstances and if any aspects of the agenda might be altered when the wicked seducer also happened to be the boss. As they drove along in silence, she began to fantasise, with a degree of excitement, about what she imagined she would soon experience and how best she might conduct herself. Margaret was not bothered by her part in the impending physical exchanges of which, in any case, she had only a sketchy, second or third-hand knowledge. It was her intention to be entirely passive and rely upon the expertise of Mr Noonan, welcoming him as her tutor and, in a sense, physical therapist. She was far more concerned about how to address him during the affray.

At first she considered that it would be worldly and sophisticated to address him as "Patrick", to his face as in "Where shall we lie down, Patrick?" or "Is that nice, Patrick?" but, perhaps wisely, soon discarded the idea. Mr Noonan would surely disapprove, she thought, since such familiarity might well lead to a breakdown in discipline at the office. In any case, she doubted that he had ever been one of those romantic souls who read the novels to be found on the shelves of the average corner shop. On the other hand, once he was actively engaged and also immediately after the event, if the indescribable pleasure of it all did not render her speechless, she could always both retain her dignity and show her partner due respect by calling him "sir" or even Mr Noonan, as she was accustomed to do at work. A formal, even controlled, turn of phrase such as "That was divine, Mr Noonan" or "I am forever in your debt, sir" might work well in theory. Margaret decided against that approach too, dismissing it as probably being one that the maidservant of a protestant landowner might adopt when waylaid by him in the laundry or pantry of his great house. Furthermore, since she was not a Quaker nor living in the seventeenth century, use of the terms "thee" and "thou" could be ruled out too. In any case, such formality would surely be inappropriate given the basic nature of what would pass between them after they left the car.

Of course, the gallant, pragmatic and experienced Mr Noonan was untroubled by any of these thoughts and so it happened that a very simple programme was followed. When they spoke at all, neither of them used any name, title nor term of affection, getting by instead with useful, neutral words such as "you", "your" and, it being Ireland around 1960, "yourself". A sort of temporary equality between unequals was thus achieved but the intimacy that followed was kept strictly within anatomical and physiological boundaries as P Noonan had always intended it to be.

Mr Noonan turned off the Old Military Road at an open gate, driving a hundred yards along a rough track and then across the scrub to a flat area partly obscured from view by a dense wild shrubbery of heather and furze. He parked the car and extinguished his cigarette. There was little or no passing traffic at the time and they were, in any case, hidden from the road by the many bushes and trees about them. He stretched across to open the door for her and then went to the boot and retrieved a well-worn tartan rug that he spread on the uneven ground a few yards from the car. He kept on his jacket but unbuttoned it to reveal a fine pair of red and green patterned braces supporting his grey trousers which extended to perhaps two inches above his brown lace-up shoes.

Given the apparent ease with which he had found his way to this secluded spot, Margaret wondered how often he had been there and with whom. Perhaps with Peggy Murray? It crossed her mind briefly that this breezy scrubland was unlikely to be where many of the great lovers of history would have chosen to take eager young maidens ripe for deflowering.

Nevertheless, she was reassured, even pleased, that Patrick Noonan was familiar with his surroundings and was obviously in command of the situation. After all, her first priority was to take a walk down the primrose path escorted by an experienced guide in whom she had confidence; exactly where he chose to explore her hidden potential was a matter of lesser importance.

Lighting another cigarette, Mr Noonan knelt on the edge of the blanket, first playing with his braces and then indicating to Margaret what she should do next. She undid the buttons of her overcoat and lay down, hitching up her dress to just above her knees. He looked pleased that she had some grasp of the general situation and, leaving his cigarette alight on a nearby rock, joined her. She noticed then that the profile of his trouser-front was beginning to change shape and increasingly take on the appearance of a rug beneath which a small animal, perhaps a kitten or puppy, moved at play. She looked away quickly lest he notice the scrutiny of his trouser gusset and consider her unduly bold for a virginal Catholic girl. She thought that, as a decently married Irishman, he might well enthusiastically embrace adultery but would surely not wish to blot his copybook by being intimate with someone who was brazenly forward. Of course, he might not be that fastidious at all and perhaps would not seek absolution from his priest for carnal sins committed with Margaret or anyone else, be they willing accomplices or not. At this point she stopped speculating and tried to concentrate on the matter in hand, as it were.

There was a fine blue sky above with just a few clouds blowing across in the evening mountain breeze.

No kisses were exchanged and the unromantic and, by now, impatient Mr Noonan seemed rapidly to forget all but his own intentions. He pulled Margaret's dress up above her waist before stripping off her knickers, dislodging one of her shoes in the process, and discarding the undergarment rather carelessly in the direction of some heather nearby. She was becoming more excited, mostly because of the impudence and wickedness inherent in lying with her boss but also because of her pressing desire to be introduced, without further delay, to the mysterious joys she had heard of. Indeed, there was no delay but neither was there any joy or much mystery, either.

Supporting his own weight on knees and elbows, he set about the main business of the moment without words or caresses. Whilst indulging himself, he seemed in a different world, indifferent to the girl beneath him and to whatever risks might be inherent in taking his pleasure. His exertions made him slightly breathless but, mercifully, he did not suffer any paroxysms of smoker's cough. Margaret lay unmoving and unmoved, still excited but with no sensation to indicate that the rapture she had been expecting was close at hand.

There was a strong aroma of tobacco emanating from Mr Noonan as he panted away. To avoid this, she looked over his shoulder and towards her feet which she could see in the air above his waist, one foot still encased in a bright red, high-heeled shoe. They moved slightly with each of his lunges and she suppressed a giggle at the thought that the red shoe might be spotted waving about and be interpreted as a distress signal by anyone who happened to be walking on the hillside some distance away. As it happened, the rapidity of Margaret's passage from virginity to womanhood was such that the red shoe waved for no more than thirty seconds and was probably seen by no creature more sentient than a hawk or a stray sheep.

Disappointed that there was little, if any, positive sensation associated with Mr Noonan's efforts, Margaret forgot the shoe and began to think of the euphemisms for her current activity which she had come across when reading about the subject in the few sources she could find. "Coupling" was one such word and she had consulted the Oxford English Dictionary to try and understand how it had come to be used in this way. There she had found that coupling was defined as "a connection between two oscillating systems, causing one to oscillate when the other does". "Oscillation" itself was described as movement to-and-fro between two points – not a good description, Margaret reflected; she felt herself to be most certainly more oscillated against than oscillating.

She was surprised, though not by any means crestfallen, when after perhaps two-dozen movements back and forth, the mighty Mr Noonan exhaled forcefully, grunted several times as if in pain and then withdrew himself rather abruptly, leaving her slightly damp and somewhat unimpressed by his brief incursion. She wondered whether she had been short-changed or if losing one's virginity was always bound to be an anti-climax. Mr Noonan might have moved a lot but the earth, most decidedly, had not. Perhaps he was simply not one of the great lovers of the twentieth, or any other, century.

Once he had disengaged, Patrick Noonan showed no further interest in Margaret. He tucked away his now redundant extremity and adjusted his trousers, buttoning his flies and stretching his braces over his shoulders once more. He lit another cigarette and walked over to the car. She stood up, retrieved and put on her undergarment after brushing away a few shreds of scratchy undergrowth and a small spider normally resident in the heather, pulled down her dress and buttoned her coat before following him. He made no comment, just sat behind the wheel looking slightly glum as men sometimes do after indulging themselves, and left her to open the car door for herself. She sat in the passenger seat, reflecting that, in spite of her new status, she felt neither delighted nor defiled and was still largely ignorant not only of the configuration of male and female working parts but also of how they could best be employed.

After a few years, Margaret could not remember whether they spoke much on the trip back to Dublin. Certainly Mr Noonan made no effort to find out what she had made of her experience and did not thank her for allowing him access or comment upon his own enjoyment of their brief adventure. Margaret, for her part, made no comment about his failure to impress her; with little knowledge, she rightly felt unqualified to judge whether his performance was, in the great scheme of things, good, bad or indifferent. Her own response was one of indifference, even to the extent that she wondered if her friends had lied to her, or at least greatly exaggerated, the joys of sex. Perhaps in his silence Mr Noonan was meditating upon the possible consequences of Ireland being an obedient and condom-free Roman Catholic country. Even so, there was nothing awkward in the situation and Margaret was delivered to the end of her road as if nothing unusual had taken place between them that evening, as though she had simply been given a lift home after working late.

The next day was the start of her new status as a woman of the world, or so Margaret thought, the banality of her coming-of-age notwithstanding. She wondered whether Mr Noonan might in future invite her to his basement office when Peggy was away and ravish her on his desk, or perhaps just speak to her with slightly less formality now that they had passed her important landmark together. Perhaps he might become more expert and patient in his ministrations to her and then be able to bring her to that climax of physical pleasure and delight of which she had heard.

She would ask Peggy if it was really called an "organism".

There was no sign of Mr Noonan when she sat down at her desk that next morning. At about 12am he came up to the typists' office and walked over to Margaret who smiled, hoping perhaps for some sort of acknowledgement or a friendly word from him.

"Miss Hogan, will you type a letter for me please?" he said, handing her a handwritten draft. So she was put firmly back in her place, well down the office pecking order and, to her disappointment, was never invited to join him along the primrose path again.

Margaret was amused when she looked back on all this in later years. She changed her course in life and became an assistant to doctors and nurses at a large city hospital. There she soon learned and understood that most men, driven by testosterone, regard the sex act as (no puns intended) a stand-alone end in itself. A man's view seemed to be that sex should ideally involve no personal commitment, at least not by the male protagonist, and very seldom be the prelude to a more significant relationship. Request followed by conquest and no subsequent inquest and (particularly) no bequest.

Once experience had taught her this, it became clear that a wise woman should always take this ingrained male attitude into consideration and either exploit it to her own advantage or at the very least treat the devout protestations of men with grave suspicion. Good advice still.

15. RANDOM EVENTS, MIRACLES AND THIN PLACES

The original Celts were story-tellers, firm believers in magic and the custodians of legends and mystical beliefs. A few of the ancient traditions have survived down the years and at least one of them, a belief in the existence of "thin places", still survives amongst some people to this day. This concept was mentioned and expanded upon in *Pardonable Offences*. The basic notion is simply that there can be moments in our banal, otherwise routine, human lives when what we experience as reality suddenly approaches the mysterious, unseen and ultimately ineffable kingdom of God and his angels. Such an event might occur in a sacred building, a forest glade, mountains or the open countryside, or simply be inspired by the words of another person. One translation of the original descriptions of thin places was that they were to be found where the natural and the supernatural are "knitted together". Often all too briefly.

The English language is one with an almost inexhaustible vocabulary and, to everyone's confusion, attaches more than a single meaning to many of the words in common use. Habitually rational individuals might well regard thin places as imaginary and most people who have found themselves in such places would have difficulty explaining their experiences, especially to a clever, cynical non-believer. That being the case, it might be useful to define and apply some of the words that are used in any conversation relating to this subject

The word "idea" can mean "fantasy" or "any conception existing in the mind as a result of mental understanding, awareness or activity". Or then again, an idea "exists independently of all other things and from which all other things derive". So basically an idea is what we think and does not mean the same as the word "truth", though it might well be the truth some or most of the time. We may "have the right idea" or, on the other hand, have "ideas beyond our station".

Reality is defined as "the state of being real" or "something that exists independently of ideas concerning it." So an idea could be remote from reality but presumably, as with any hypotheses, any idea might or might not subsequently prove to be correct and therefore very much real. There is a clear intersection between those words and how they are used.

Something imaginary is not real although it might have its origins in an idea. And an idea is sometimes real. Imagination has been described as "the faculty for forming mental images or ideas that are not actually present in the senses". That definition assumes that the mind is not purely a sensory organ. So one might prefer to say, "Imagination is the faculty of producing ideal creations consistent with reality – as in literature or art.".

It would probably be neurotic and could become obsessional to try and apply the words real, idea, fantasy, imaginary and imagination to the subject when attempting to explain what occurs when one enters a "thin place". Real emotions are involved in those that find themselves in these places, and emotion is not a subject that the average neuroscientist would attempt to explain at a cellular level. It is clear that thin places are not real insofar as they cannot be recognised from a passing car window, photographed, copied, measured or recorded by any objective scientific means or adequately described by music or poetry. Perhaps, as with another unscientific entity, human love, the last two options of music and poetry might at least transport one in the right direction but no further than that.

Faith, even in the obvious, is very much anathema to the demi-psychotic priests of the modern woke sect. Therefore, taking all these points into consideration, it is best simply to report the experiences of people who believe they found a thin place and to leave interpretation to the reader.

A miracle has been defined as an extraordinary event taken as a sign of God's supernatural power. Then again, the word is used in common speech to describe an extremely outstanding or unusual event, thing or accomplishment. It might be presumptuous to state as much, but true miracles (that is to say, actual events that do not involve magic or hypnotic suggestion) must surely occur within the laws of nature. Which raises at least two questions:

1. Who made the intricate laws of nature (physics, chemistry, time, light and space *inter alia*)?
2. Is it purely random coincidence that brings about the useful mobilisation of natural forces at precisely the right time and place for a miracle to occur? Can that be proven?

Life-changing events are associated with chance meetings quite often, one suspects. However, what might simply be regarded as no more than "good luck" by some could easily be interpreted quite differently by others and even considered miraculous when that "good luck" intervenes at just the right moment to save a life or heal a broken heart. A few examples follow of ordinary people finding themselves unexpectedly, but mercifully, in "thin places".

More than five decades ago I took my small family to spend a long weekend at a seaside resort on the Natal southern coast. We were resting for a few days before setting off on an adventure that would see us living in Woodstock, Oxfordshire, whilst I completed postgraduate training at the famous university nearby. Walking on the beach one morning, I met an old school friend who was staying with his wife and children at a different hotel in the resort. Nothing particularly strange in such a meeting, even though we had last spoken at high school about 12 years earlier. Coincidence.

Certainly chance must have been involved. However, at just that time, my friend Ewen had travelled some 1000 miles from Rhodesia, where medical facilities were good but limited, in the hope of finding a doctor who could offer hope for his little daughter Jean, who was dying of an auto-immune kidney disease. He had, again by chance, chosen to stay on the coast rather than in town and happened, surely for no good reason, to walk along the beach in my direction at just the right time. Or perhaps I was walking in his direction.

As it happened, I had recently written and passed the South African examination for internists (specialist physicians) and was preparing to enter the more famous British equivalent later in the same year. By accident and long before the advent of Google, Ewen found himself in the company of a sort of (very temporary) living reference library of medicine and its recent advances. He explained what he was doing in Natal and provided a very clear history of his daughter's illness. It was a relatively simple matter to refer him to a Durban kidney specialist whom I knew and who had just lately returned from a refresher course in the United States.

The little girl responded to the newly developed treatment the physician provided and is still alive and well more than 55 years on. All those chance events came together to bring about a wonderful outcome. Not just for a little girl but also for her desperately worried parents for whom the events were evidence enough that thin places exist and that sometimes, perhaps only for the desperate and the humble, a veil between the natural world and the arcane is breeched.

Such episodes are not really all that uncommon during the course of a long life.

My home in Ireland is about a quarter mile from the Blackwater, whose tidal waters provide space for salmon fishermen and poachers, riverbank walks for local residents and an ideal habitat for otters and mink. Vanessa, my elder daughter with a background in medical science, would walk her two large dogs along the riverside fairly regularly during late spring, summer and early autumn. Once the heavy winter rains came, fishing spots would be scarce and the paths became impassable. So the dogs were taken to the forest nearby instead, where they could chase rabbits and dash about more or less unhindered.

Vanessa's mother died peacefully at home one summer's morning after a long period of suffering, borne with uncommon courage. Throughout her illness, she was given the best of loving support by compassionate hospice staff and by her own family. Anyone who has ever experienced the bitterness of a real bereavement will understand how painful it can be, especially when one is a member of a social group that has been taught to try and hide even the most powerful of emotions.

One afternoon, soon after her mother's death, Vanessa took her two large dogs for a walk along the river path. Miserable and bereft, she asked aloud – there being no one else about – where her mother might be and if she was safe and secure. Within a few seconds, two fully grown otters appeared on the way, about 20 yards ahead. They sat up in the middle of the path, regarding her and the two dogs with interest and no sign of fear. Astonishingly the dogs, that would normally have chased and attacked the otters, simply remained at her side as if this were the most normal of experiences. Otters were hunted along the Blackwater until a mere generation ago by the kind of half-finished morons that love blood sports. They are shy creatures and avoid humans and, of course, dogs.

So here was another example of a rare unexpected event that happened at a critical time. Strange and opportune but it involved living creatures and a setting that were real and obedient to the laws of nature. This experience had a soothing effect and brought peace of mind when it was most needed. How odd that the otters and the dogs acted as if to some sort of script. Was it just chance? Had they wandered into a thin place? Was it a miracle fashioned for one unhappy soul?

During the last few years of my wife Pat's life we would visit New England every autumn, go hiking with close friends and enjoy the marvellous display of fall colours by the broad-leafed trees that grow there in such profusion. The final trip, in May 2011, was particularly memorable. We had our first and only close encounter with a moose, witnessed a wonderful performance of *Cavalleria Rusticana* and ate, drank and laughed with old friends. Best of all, we sat for a while at a favourite spot near Colby Hill Inn, beside the Contoocook River that runs through Henniker, New Hampshire. We found acorns that had fallen from the red oaks (*Quercus Rubra*) that grow in that area and today, 12 years later as I write, two healthy trees grown from these acorns stand in the lower meadow at Ballinadine, about fifteen feet tall.

At the time, naturally enough, we had no idea that the haunting Intermezzo from Mascagni's opera would soon be played at Pat's funeral, still less that something strange would happen on my return to the Henniker riverbank, just over a year after her death.

No doubt there are a number of ways of dealing with grief. Mine was to find consolation in revisiting favourite places, silent prayer, occasional tears and the fellowship of good friends. In autumn 2012, a break in New England seemed to be the answer. During that trip, I went back to Colby Hill Inn and drove the short distance along the river to the place on the bank where we had sat so often before. As ever, the trees were utter perfection, the clear waters ran by at speed over the rapids and the only sound, other than that of the river itself, was an occasional bird-call. It was beautiful and comfortable and I sat on a rock alone, absorbing the lovely scene. Not unexpectedly, self-pity being what it is, sadness returned and, with it, resentment that life should have taken such a turn. Where then was there any evidence of the peace of God?

An answer was not long in coming. As I turned to go back to my car, my path was partly blocked by a large shrub, a Mountain Laurel. Strangely, it had not been that obvious when I walked down to the bank of the Contoocook and yet there it was before me. Stranger still, for this is a native shrub that normally flowers in May and June, it was radiant, almost completely covered in delicate white blossoms.

This whole experience was counter-intuitive, of course, and could have been some sort of hallucination. On returning to the spot a year or two later, there was no sign of any Mountain Laurel, white or otherwise.

The occasional cynical botanist might point out that plants have been known to flower out of season and, furthermore, that however perfect the tiny blooms of Kalmia latifolia might be, all parts of the plant are poisonous to both man and animals. Perhaps this was no more than an extrasensory nudge, a reminder to accept life as it is, rough or smooth.

Since the dawn of time, many, if not most, human societies have believed in magic, oracles, soothsayers and general mumbo-jumbo. Presumably these superstitions arise partly because half of us have intelligence quotients well below par and partly because contemplating the astonishing truths of our existence, lost in the cosmos, can be terrifying. Better to block reality by drugs, fanatical interest in football, say, or subscribing to some cult led by a dysfunctional pop-star or charismatic lunatic centred on patriotism or some *faux* religion.

Yet we only have to slow down, take a few deep breaths and consider the physical world about us to realise, like Plato, that we really know nothing.

Surely an all-powerful creator would use the very laws of nature, now and again, to fulfil His ineffable purposes? A tsunami to part the Red Sea, perhaps; an earthquake to bring down the walls of Jericho and a bolt of lightning to save old William Leary's family from the Pondomisi ambush in the African wilds.

Just considering a few simple facts should destroy our hubris and fill us with wonder. Consider that hundreds of biochemical reactions occur in each living cell every hour of the day, that a hummingbird has a heartrate of 500 to 1200 beats per minute when active and only 50 when asleep or that a beam of light, under certain physical conditions, can carry an infinite amount of information.

So, should we really continue to tell the world that men can be masters of their fate and captains of their souls?

16. FLANDERS FIELDS

It is a matter of record that there was something of a Celtic revival in Ireland towards the end of the nineteenth century when the country still formed part of Queen Victoria's Great Britain. Politicians, poets, playwrights and others in the public eye began to tell their countrymen that they were heirs to a great and ancient culture, separate and by no means inferior to that of their English masters. A sense of pride in the native culture was revived and patriotism began to grow apace. A majority of the population were content to support the idea of Home Rule, within the British Empire, whilst a significant minority were in favour of an independent Irish republic, to be secured by violence if necessary. Thus, at the start of the Great War in 1914, the people of Ireland were divided in their attitudes to their rulers in London and to supporting them in this conflict. Tens of thousands of Irishmen joined the British forces, some because of the promise that Home Rule would be Ireland's reward but also for a variety of other reasons, not excluding simple poverty. A small number of ultra-nationalists plotted revolution at home. Some families, such as my own, took the view that the English were slightly embarrassing, sometimes annoying, relatives and, as distant cousins, should be supported when outsiders intervened in family matters. As my father once said, "We don't want people interfering with OUR enemies." Not really an attitude that was that easy to understand, perhaps. After all, the main belligerents were both led by descendants of the famine Queen – Victoria – who was not ethnically British at all. Most of the European rulers were, like Victoria, the descendants of a number of inbred aristocratic German families. Furthermore, the allied generals were mostly queer and peculiar, if brave, Englishmen who had nothing much in common with the Irish volunteers or, indeed, their own men.

In 1916, while some 170,000 Irishmen were serving at the front, the Easter Rising unexpectedly took place in Dublin. Shambolic to an extent that would do credit to any modern day political party, the rebellion resulted in the deaths of far more innocent Irish civilians than British soldiers or nationalist insurgents. This event prompted a brutal and typically short-sighted response by the British. The leaders of the revolt were treated as ruthlessly as cowards at the front, court martialled without benefit of adequate legal support, and sentenced to death. Appeals for mercy by compassionate members of the British establishment, together with a prophetic warning issued in the London parliament by an Irish loyalist MP, failed to stop the executions. They were taken to Kilmainham gaol and shot. The stupid and dictatorial behaviour this entailed made instant martyrs of the rebels and turned the bulk of the Irish population against the Crown. Enthusiasm for the war against Kaiser Wilhelm evaporated and Irish soldiers in Flanders and France found that they no longer had the moral support of their countrymen. More shameful events followed.

After the armistice in November 1918, Irish soldiers returned home to a muted welcome. Most were still young and many had been blinded or severely wounded in the fighting. They might have expected a gentle reception and, at the least, simple human kindness and warmth. Instead, they found it unwise to mention their service in what was regarded as the British army, irrespective of the motives that might have led them to enlist originally. At least one Irish hero, Michael O'Leary VC, and many other former soldiers felt obliged to leave the country and try to forget Ireland forever. Being a soldier had become a political issue that was raised repeatedly by the new republicans. These hard, uncompromising men preferred to ignore the sad fact that their own folk, like thousands of other young men from Germany and the British, Austro-Hungarian and Ottoman Empires had gone to war in good faith, believing the self-serving lies of those in authority.

As the poet Rudyard Kipling, who lost his son John, put it:

If any question why we died
Tell them, because our fathers lied.

Like most of the frontline soldiers, the young Irishmen suffered greatly and, in about 40,000 cases, died pointlessly during the terrible, demonic conflict that was World War I. At home the situation became worse in the years of insurrection and strife that followed the armistice of 1918 and for many decades thereafter most families kept their own sad stories to themselves, unable properly to mourn their dead and afraid, even ashamed, to admit kinship to these heroic youngsters. Two generations later, the lost men and boys, the youngest of whom was only 14, were all but forgotten until the brave and controversial journalist Kevin Myers raised the issue and kept at it doggedly until, at last, their sacrifice was finally recognised by proper memorials on Irish soil.

I first met Vivien Ann when we worked in the same concern in South Africa. I knew very little about her at the time beyond the fact that she came from Ireland, my great-grandfather's country, which I had visited only once. After a year or two, she left Africa and contact between us was lost until about 40 years later when we met by chance in England and, in time, became close friends.

When speaking of our family backgrounds one day, it emerged that her maternal grandfather, Private James Patrick Rowan, had been killed during the Great War and that he was buried somewhere near the French battlefields. He had been born in a tiny hamlet called Straide, near Castlebar in the county Mayo, and enlisted in an Irish regiment at the start of the war. In 1917, he had lost his life somewhere in either Flanders or France. The immediate family did not know where he lay buried and her parents had never said much about him. Further tragedy had followed his death. His widow, an Englishwoman, and son both perished in the great Spanish influenza pandemic of 1918, leaving his orphaned daughters to be raised by relatives in England.

Various internet websites provide military information and so, knowing the dead man's full names and place of birth, it was possible to find details of his regiment and number, rank, date of death and precisely where he was buried in Flanders. Armed with this information, we travelled to Ypres (or Ieper) in Belgium, in search of an ordinary, almost forgotten, man, loved in life by his wife and family long ago but cruelly and disgracefully deserted and rejected in death by people of his own blood for almost a century.

It was a fine summer's morning when we were driven out to the relatively small military graveyard where the man from Mayo and several hundred of his comrades, officers and other ranks, lay together beneath perfectly tended lawns. As with all such places, cared for by the Commonwealth War Graves organisation, the cemetery was immaculate. A garden rather than a mortuary. The graves were arranged in neat rows, each white headstone carved with the cap badge of the dead man's regiment, usually recording his name, age, date of death and sometimes also bearing a few sad words in witness to a mother's grief. Many of the graves were those of unidentified casualties, nameless but with the moving inscription: "A soldier of the Great War. Known unto God." The names of more than 50,000 such men, "the missing", are inscribed on the walls of the wonderful Menin Gate in Ypres city, where the Last Post sounds every evening in memory of them and all the allied war dead. Would that the Irish had been consistent with their own reputation for sentimentality a century ago and honoured these men as they deserved.

We found where he lay in Kemmel Chateau Military Cemetery without difficulty and placed a small wooden cross and poppy on the grave which was marked with his name and the insignia of the Connaught Rangers. As we stood there in silence beside the grave, contemplating the wickedness and futility of that war, a butterfly appeared as if it had been specially summoned. It came to us suddenly, soundlessly, and seemingly from nowhere before alighting on the top of the headstone. For what it may be worth it was of a variety commonly known as the Painted Lady (*Vanessa cardui*) which arrives in Europe each spring from sub-Saharan Africa, returning six months and several generations later to the south. After perhaps a minute or two, during which we were rooted to the spot, thinking we were caught up in a dream, the butterfly fluttered away as silently and quickly as it had first appeared from the sky.

During the next half hour, as we walked about in sunshine and read the names on other tombstones, we did not see so much as a single butterfly of any variety. Not in the cemetery nor in the extensive open fields nearby. Much later, we learnt that the tiny Painted Ladies may fly, in large groups, up to 1,500 feet above the earth, making them invisible to the unaided human eye. Perhaps the butterfly of Ypres had come down to investigate from a formation flying at such a height.

There are more than 150 World War I British cemeteries in Flanders and, including all combatants, perhaps 100,000 graves. Just over one thousand headstones stand in Kemmel Chateau Military Cemetery set in several acres of lawns, flowers and trees. Yet a single, bright butterfly appeared just as we arrived at that one, particular grave. Is it really magical thinking to believe that this was not just by chance?

In the company of that brightly coloured little creature, wherever it came from, we stood beside a grave at Kemmel Chateau, Ypres, to remember and pray for Private James Patrick Rowan, number 2629, 6th Battalion Connaught Rangers.

On that particular day, the peaceful cemetery was a very thin place indeed. The material world and that which is unseen were knitted together. Whether this was the product of imagination, coincidence or supernatural powers remains hidden. But we chose to think that there was a force at work that could not be explained and that brought with it, love, beauty and consolation. *"Blessed are they that mourn for they shall be comforted."*

In times of emotional turmoil, people sometimes feel that they are supported, for better or worse, by an unseen presence – what "clever" cynics might call *an imaginary friend*. Perhaps so, and no doubt psychologists can offer various explanations for such experiences, confidently spouting impressive sounding nonsense from sources within their almost entirely theoretical discipline to try to explain what is fundamentally inexplicable. Nevertheless, delusions and hallucinations aside, unexplained forces do appear to intervene now and then, in strange ways. When this happens, a quite ordinary place can become very thin indeed.

17. PEOPLE AND CATS WITH NAMES

Ireland was the birthplace of my great grandfather, William Leary. A few years before the famine, he enlisted in the British Army at a barracks near his home in Naas, County Kildare, and was sent to South Africa with his regiment. He lived there for 60 years and never returned home. In 1990, I came back to Ireland with part of the family. He was never to know that some of his great-great-great-grandchildren, including one named William, would be Irish and attend schools and universities not all that far from Naas.

Ireland is a beautiful and welcoming place to its own and also to most strangers, but is distinguished, for better or worse, by a good few practices and attitudes that seem unfortunate or, at the least, strange to people accustomed to a different pattern of behaviour. For example, no one should confuse the average friendly Irishman with the run-of-the-mill, middle-class Englishman. Some of the former are liable to be what the Irish themselves term "chancers" and many of the latter, in my experience, sensibly prefer the company of dogs and cats to that of their fellow countrymen.

Soon after we came back to Ireland, we noticed that, whilst most of the rural Irish clearly loved horses and treated their working sheepdogs quite well, it was unusual for a family cat to have its own name or be encouraged to live inside the house. A mat on the floor near the kitchen stove or by the fireside might occasionally be provided. Some of our newly made Irish friends were even afraid of cats or seemed to believe that their self-contained ways indicated that they might be in league with Satan himself. They would go out of their way to avoid them and took no special care to spare them if they wandered in front of traffic on some country road.

This sad and ignorant approach upsets me still. I learned to love cats from an early age, perhaps two or three, when I would play on the floor with my parents' much adored pet cat, a pitch-black fellow named JC Smuts. Every cat that I knew as both child and adult lived inside, slept on the beds and was named after a politician, entertainer, sporting hero or friend. Since my background was that of somewhat reserved, Protestant conformity, I wondered if the relative lack of interest in cats shown by my Irish cousins had its origins in the Roman Curia, whose allegedly infallible teachings apparently included the unimaginative ruling that animals were without soul. In my opinion, an absurd view without biblical basis and one that appears to ignore the transcendent beauty and intricate design of even the smallest of living creatures, let alone sentient animals such as cats and dogs. My personal heresy is to believe that humans are not just bodies that have immortal souls but that they, in common with animals, are souls that occupy perishable flesh and blood.

In the old African British colonies, black people who went to the mission stations for one purpose or another were often given baptismal names that were easy on the English tongue. The names of more or less obscure Old Testament figures were quite often favoured even if they made little sense in the minds of the colonised people. Other, non-biblical names that were familiar to the British were also popular and a Zulu or Pondo boy might answer to a puzzling (to him) name such as Wellington, Milton or, famously, Nelson. Both sets of names sounded faintly ridiculous when they were coupled with the proud name of a Zulu, Xhosa or Sotho clan but they were chosen for the convenience of the white ruling class, most of whom were incapable of mastering the pronunciation of words that included various click-sounds which were quite beyond their vocal range. Slightly behind the scenes, every Nguni or Sotho person also had another name; not Daniel, Bismarck, Enoch, Zephaniah or Rebecca but one that meant something in their own language and had some cultural significance. These might often be clan names, words of gratitude or hopes for the future, or names that described the appearance or perceived early nature of the child. How lovely to name a child "Sipho", meaning "gift", or "Sibongile", meaning "we give thanks".

As noted elsewhere, the great Zulus where we lived were in the habit of bestowing secret names upon individual white people with whom they came into regular contact. Often these names were descriptive, even humorous, and referred to the posture, physique or habits of their target; thus, "he who looks down", "the fat man", "head in the clouds", "red face", "the one who sweats a lot", "the one who shouts".

In his poem, *Naming of Cats*, TS Eliot revealed that cats have their own secret names but these are known only to themselves and never to humans. If that is so, perhaps rural Irish kitties, knowing this secret, are quite content to remain otherwise nameless or to respond to whatever name humans might give them, always provided that food is supplied. Certainly every cat I ever lived with, and they have numbered perhaps two dozen over the years, knew the name that he or she had been given, and came when called whether to dinner or to bed.

People who neither know nor love cats tend to be soon converted if they are introduced to a particular one with character. So it is with people in Ireland, once the first barriers of ignorance and superstition are removed.

There are many stories of feline devotion that suggest these animals are sensitive to many things, not least the joy, suffering or sadness they are able to detect in their human companions. It is worth recounting just one example of this sensitivity, an event that I witnessed in my own home.

During spring of 2000, our beloved ginger tom, Garfield, was killed by falling masonry at the side of our 200-year-old house. For months we grieved for him and swore never to let another cat into our hearts. I was so badly affected at the time that I required medical treatment for a reactive cardiac irregularity.

One afternoon, an ordinary black and white tom, a tuxedo cat to Americans, appeared from behind the shrubbery beside the lawn where I was at work. The cat, perhaps a year or two old, walked straight across to where I was, on my knees weeding, and announced his intention of moving in by stepping up to my lap, butting me with his head and purring loudly. An old hand in these matters, I knew that he had come looking for a forever home and that it would be useless to resist. So the newcomer was adopted, neutered, vaccinated and named Felix.

He became a favourite of Patricia, my wife, upon whose side of the bed he liked to snooze before breakfast every day. An expensive cat, we saw him through a few illnesses, not least an intestinal obstruction caused by swallowing a large rodent head first. We loved him over the years as four or five other cats came and went. Given to much back-chat, Felix always kept his human friends informed as to his whereabouts in the house or gardens. He never divulged his secret name, of course.

About ten years later, Patricia became terminally ill. Felix seemed to sense the change in her and kept watch from a chair at her bedside from which he would disappear only for meals and the occasional calls of nature. He was not in the room when she died but came in soon afterwards and quietly took up his position on the bedside chair beside her silent form. Her body was taken away soon afterwards but Felix remained on his chair, on guard as it were, perhaps sensing something in another dimension. There he stayed, neither purring nor communicating with anyone who entered the room – a picture of misery, his head bowed. Perhaps he prayed, who can say? It was three days before he could be persuaded to leave his post and even then he had to be picked up, cradled and carried from the room. No doubt he sensed the sorrow in the house and reacted to it; or possibly there was much more to it all. Nobody will ever know.

Felix lived for another seven years, giving all of us much affection and taking great joy in a life spent eating, sleeping in the sun or on a well-appointed bed and going outside now and then to cull the small rodents that lived in a grassy bank near the house. During his final two years, a partial obstruction of his gullet meant that he could no longer eat solid food and so, in keeping with the unspoken agreement decent people make with their pets, he was cared for and fed at home, often by hand, on a liquid diet. It was no more than a quid pro quo for the pleasure he had given the family and, in particular, the devotion he had shown his dying mistress years before. Over time, he gradually became weaker, looking for and finding his human friends in his final hour and dying quietly whilst we sat in tears beside him. Felix was put to rest forever beneath beautiful flowering shrubs, close to a small pond where he used to watch the tadpoles swimming in the spring or drink the water that came down to the garden from a mountain stream.

Was that really all? Did he simply perish, a body with no soul, a tuxedo cat with no more than an arbitrary name given to him by humans?

Perhaps it was the end, but no one with any heart at all or a belief in a loving Creator could think so.

ABOUT THE AUTHOR

The author is a retired physician and university professor turned horticulturalist and humourist.

He was born in South Africa where he was an athletics Full Blue at university, followed the Australians Ron Clarke (1956) and Herb Elliott (1957) as the world fastest junior miler, and qualified as a medical doctor in 1961. He later graduated DPhil at Oxford University, earned a DSc degree and became a Fellow of colleges of physicians in three countries. He pursued an international career in clinical pharmacology but spent much of his time teaching and attending to black patients in what is now Kwa-Zulu Natal. He emigrated to Ireland in 1991. He continued research work and teaching in Cork and settled in County Waterford, where he still lives.

Printed in Poland
by Amazon Fulfillment
Poland Sp. z o.o., Wrocław

29336863R00067